Home
Handyman
in
Pictures

Home Handyman in Pictures

By STEVE PRITCHARD
and BRIAN WILKINS

Published by WOLFE PUBLISHING LIMITED
10 EARLHAM STREET, LONDON WC2H 9LP
in association with INDEPENDENT TELEVISION
BOOKS LIMITED, publishers of TVTIMES

We acknowledge with thanks information and help supplied by:

Electricity Council, 1, Charing Cross, London, S.W.1.

Key Terrain Ltd., Larkfield, Maidstone, Kent.

Marley, Sevenoaks, Kent.

Cement and Concrete Association, 52, Grosvenor Gardens, London, S.W.1.

John Newton and Co., Ltd., 12, Verney Road, London, S.E.16.

Philips Electrical Ltd., Century House, Shaftesbury Avenue, London, W.C.2.

J. A. Hewetson and Co., Ltd., Marfleet, Hull.

Expandite Ltd., Western Road, Bracknell, Berks.

The Rawlplug Co., Ltd., Rawlplug House, 147, London Road, Kingston upon Thames, Surrey.

Artur Fischer (U.K.) Ltd., 41, Loverock Road, Reading, Berks.

Thorsman & Co., Ltd., Thor House, Yarrow Mill, Chorley, Lancs.

Stanley Tools Ltd., Woodside, Sheffield.

Black and Decker Ltd., Cannon Lane, Maidenhead, Berks.

SBN 7234 0545 X

Made and Printed in Great Britain
by C. Nicholls and Company Ltd.

contents

Continued overleaf

contents (continued)

before you start

With the ever-rising cost of skilled labour and materials, Do-It-Yourself has become a necessity rather than a hobby.

HOME HANDYMAN IN PICTURES has been designed so that even the least expert amateur can tackle successfully a wide range of jobs in and around the home.

The step-by-step pictures and captions take each operation through from a list of tools and materials to the finished job.

For complete success – and safety – a few simple rules must be observed:

● Read the appropriate section carefully, right through, before you start.

● Take careful note of any warnings in the text.

● When doing a job, read the individual stage caption in relation to the drawing above. Do not simply follow the pictures and skim the text.

● When using any proprietary materials or equipment, follow the manufacturer's instructions carefully.

● Keep all tools in good condition. Make sure that cutting tools are kept sharp. Apart from giving a less satisfactory result, blunt tools are far more likely to cause accidents.

● *Never* attempt any kind of electrical repair with the appliance plugged into the socket. When dealing with permanent electrical fittings, such as light sockets, first make sure that the electricity is turned off at the mains.

● If in any doubt at all about an electrical repair, do not attempt it yourself, but call in a qualified electrician.

● When using adhesives, solvents, or any substance which gives off heavy or inflammable vapours, make sure the room is well ventilated and that there are no naked lights or any heat source anywhere near.

● Be especially careful when using power tools or heat sources such as a blowlamp or soldering iron.

● Before attempting any work involving ladders, please read the section on pages 18 and 19.

*　　*　　*

With this book you should be able to reduce considerably the cost of keeping your home in good repair – and you should get a lot of interest and fun at the same time.

Tools
and
Equipment

drills and drilling

You can use many types of drills. The essential ones are the portable electric drill with attachments for carrying out jobs such as drilling, sanding, buffing, grinding and polishing, and the hand drill used mainly for metal but often for woodwork.

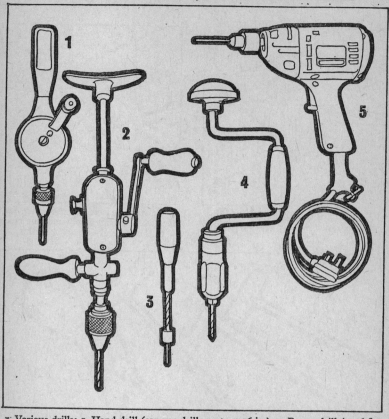

1 Various drills: *1*. Hand drill (can use drills up to 5/16 in.). *2*. Breast drill (used for heavier jobs). *3*. Push drill (for light work). *4*. Brace drill (holds a variety of bits). *5*. Electric portable drill.

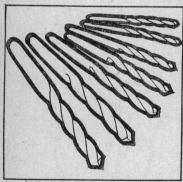

2 Twist drills used to make holes in wood or metal for screws, rivets, or bolts. High-speed twist drills range from ⅟16 in. diameter upwards.

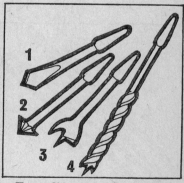

3 Types of bits used with brace: *1*. Flat headed countersink. *2*. Rose countersink. *3*. Centre bit. *4*. Twist bit.

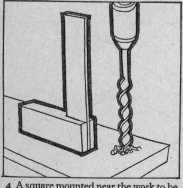

4 A square mounted near the work to be drilled helps to keep the drill at right angles to the work.

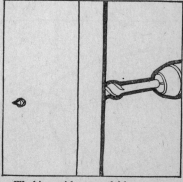

5 Working with a wood bit or auger, drill until point appears on other side, then drill from other side.

6 A masonry drill is used for drilling through walls and has a hardened tip.

7 To prevent cracks appearing on tiles when drilling apply adhesive tape to the tile and drill through this.

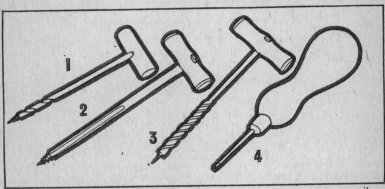

8 Some boring tools: *1*. Half twist gimlet. *2*. Shell gimlet. *3*. Auger. *4*. Bradawl.

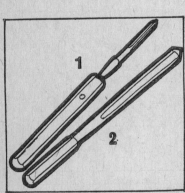

9 These are: *1*. Rawlplug tool and bit. *2*. Spade bit for masonry.

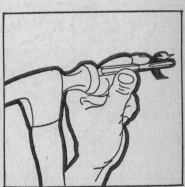

10 For a bracket hole, drive a rawlplug tool in with a hammer, at the same time rotating the tool after each stroke.

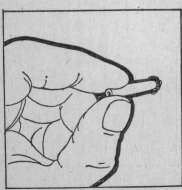

11 Now insert the correct size rawlplug for taking the screw in the hole.

12 Place the bracket hole against the wall hole and screw home firmly.

some attachments for your power drill

The versatility of the power drill and its various attachments allows you to do almost any job in the home.

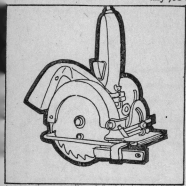

1 A circular saw attachment that can saw wood up to $1\frac{1}{4}$ in. thick. Adjustable for depth and angle of cut.

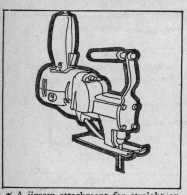

2 A jigsaw attachment for straight or intricate cuts in most materials.

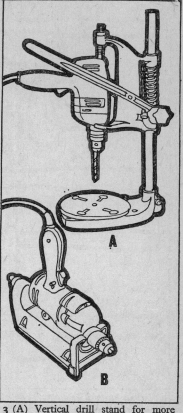

3 (A) Vertical drill stand for more accurate work. (B) Horizontal drill stand used for grinding and polishing.

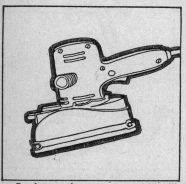

4 Sander attachment to your drill will give a smooth surface to any job.

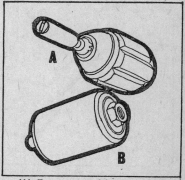

5 (A) Power screwdriver attachment. (B) Rotary hammer suitable for drilling into concrete.

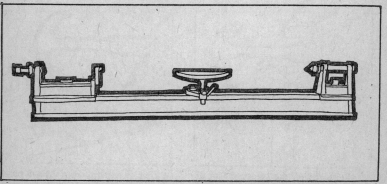

6 You can fit your drill into this lathe to give you turning and facing work, and many other operations that a lathe can give.

hammers and nails

Hammers and nails for fastening and fixing are perhaps used more than any other tools. Hammering in nails correctly can save damage to your fingers.

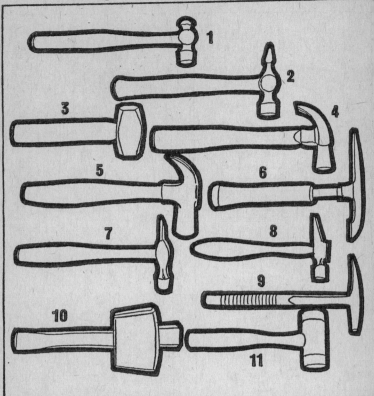

1 Various types of hammers. *1.* Ball-pein. *2.* Warrington. *3.* Club. *4.* Claw. *5.* Ripper hammer. *6.* Brick. *7.* Pattern makers. *8.* London. *9.* Upholsterers. *10* Wood mallet. *11.* Plastic soft face.

2 The correct way to hold and grip a hammer, always at the rear end.

3 Deliver the blow through the wrist, the elbow and shoulder. Start by resting the hammer on the nail then drawing it back.

4 Always deliver the hardened face of the hammer to the nail.

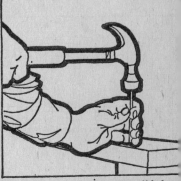

5 Using a nail set, drive the nail below the surface of the work.

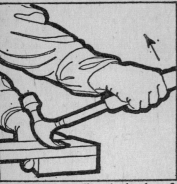

6 To extract a nail apply the claw of the hammer under the nail head and pull upwards.

7 Finish pulling when the hammer is vertical with the work.

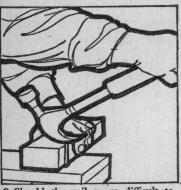

8 Should the nail prove difficult to extract, slip a piece of wood under the hammer head to give increased leverage.

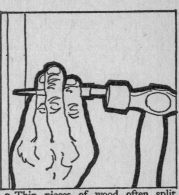

9 Thin pieces of wood often split easily. Drill a small hole to take the nail, hammer home, then sink the nail head with a punch set.

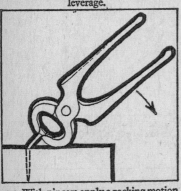

10 With pincers apply a rocking motion to pull out a stubborn nail.

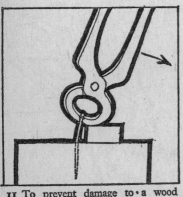

11 To prevent damage to a wood surface place a block of hardwood for the pincers to work on and to give extra leverage.

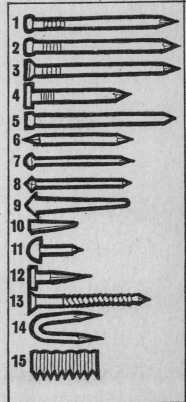

12 A selection of nails. 1. Roundwire. 2. Oval wire. 3. French nail. 4. Clout nail. 5. Masonry nail. 6. Dowel. 7. Panel pin. 8. Hardboard pin. 9. Wrought nail. 10. Picture sprig. 11. Chair nail. 12. Tack. 13. Screw nail. 14. Staple. 15. Corrugated fastener.

the use of ladders about the house

Always examine a ladder for any faults – especially if it has been borrowed or hired – and pay particular attention to the rungs before using it.

1. Always stand your ladder on firm ground. If the earth beneath is soft, make up a stout board with screwed batten as shown.

2. If the ground is uneven, place wedges of wood under one stile to act as packing.

3. Where possible lash the ladder at the top and secure it to a nearby object. A screweye in the fascia board is a good place.

4. An alternative method in soft ground is to stake firmly two posts and lash the ladder to them.

5. This is a 3-part extension ladder. When buying, always work out how long a ladder you want – single, 2-part or 3-part extension.

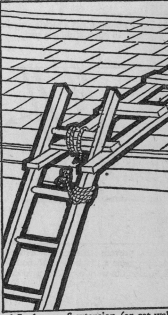

6. Lash a roof extension (or cat wall) to the main ladder as shown.

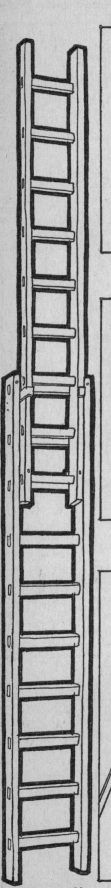

7 Here a step ladder is combined with a special type of ladder with supporting leg to make a safe working platform.

8 This is a short ladder with a screwed batten at the base combined with a step ladder, with platform to work from.

10 When working with long ladders, the distance the foot of the ladder should be from the house is a quarter of the height at the ladder top.

9 Be doubly careful when working on staircase walls and ceilings. Anchor the ladders with battens and always test the system for rigidity.

planes and chisels

Planes are used for removing and smoothing down wood. There are many types to choose from but for the handyman only three are absolutely necessary for jobs around the home – a Jack plane, block plane and smoothing plane. Chisels are used for removing sections of wood such as joints.

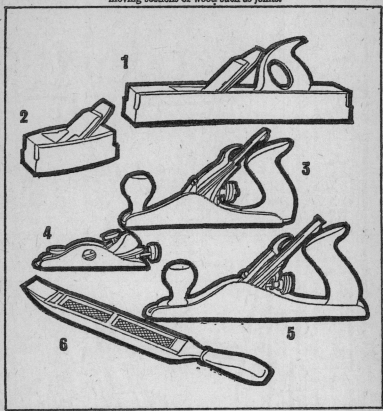

1 Types of planes: *1*. Jack plane. *2*. Smoothing plane. *3*. Adjustable metal smoothing plane. *4*. Adjustable metal block plane. *5*. Adjustable metal Jack plane. *6*. Surform tool (used for roughing work).

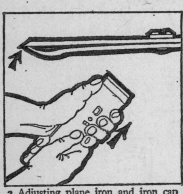

2 Adjusting plane iron and iron cap together, advance cap until its edge is just back from the cutting edge of the plane iron.

3 Hold plane iron and cap firmly together and tighten up screw as shown.

4 To push plane iron out, turn adjusting nut until blade projects through the throat and beyond the bottom of plane – not too far out.

5 To adjust evenness of shaving, sight along the bottom of the plane and move lateral adjustment lever either right or left.

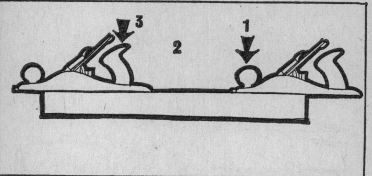

When planing start with pressure on plane knob (1). Then pressure on both knob and handle (2). Finally pressure on handle (3) at end of stroke.

Corners of the end grain of wood l break if planed right across. Always plane from corners to middle.

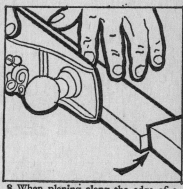

8 When planing along the edge of a piece of wood always allow a ⅜ in. overhang.

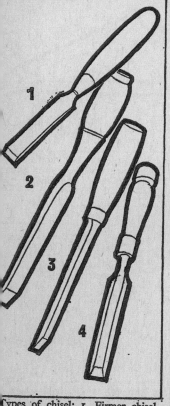

Types of chisel: *1*. Firmer chisel. Socket chisel. *3*. Mortise chisel. *4*. Firmer bevel chisel.

10 Vertical paring: control the chisel with the thumb and fingers guiding blade, whilst the shoulder provides movement on top of handle.

11 Removing a segment of wood from the groove of a housing joint with the use of chisel and mallet.

saws and sawing

The handyman has a variety of saws to choose from and it always pays to buy the best quality. How fine a cut the saw will make depends on how many teeth there are to one inch. The more teeth to the measure, the finer will be the cut.

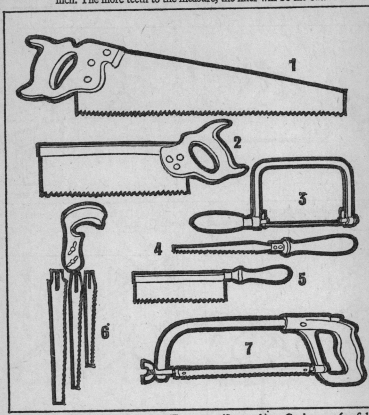

1 Some types of saw: *1.* Rip saw. *2.* Tenon saw (fine teeth). *3.* Coping saw (useful curves). *4.* Keyhold saw (used for internal cuts). *5.* Bead saw (used for small work *6.* Set of saws. *7.* Hacksaw (for cutting metal).

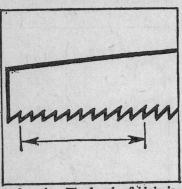

2 Saw size: The length of blade in inches and the tooth size (number of points in distance of 1 in. including those at both ends).

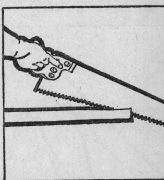

3 Start the cut by holding the saw at shallow angle on the timber in ord to see if it is in line.

4 Now hold the saw at a higher angle for ripping about 60° from the work.

5 When down sawing hold the saw a at an angle of 60° from the work.

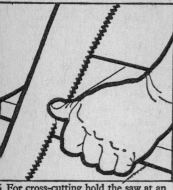

For cross-cutting hold the saw at an angle of 45° from the work. See how the thumb is guiding the saw.

7 Keep the same angle of 45° when the work is held in a vice.

Use tenon saw for smaller accurate work such as cutting joints, etc.

9 This shows the use of a coping saw for cutting irregular shapes.

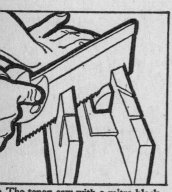

The tenon saw with a mitre block. Hold with the hand and take an angled cut through the guide slots.

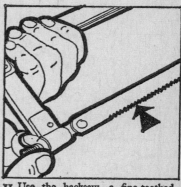

11 Use the hacksaw, a fine-toothed saw, for cutting metal. The blade is removable.

To start cutting with a hacksaw, a nick into the surface of the work to give a good start.

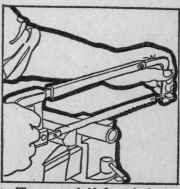

13 The correct hold for a hacksaw. Press on the forward stroke; lift off on return stroke. Blades cut only one way.

sharpening chisels and saws

New tools are supplied with perfectly ground edges but not always with sharpened edges. Oil stones and sharpening devices are necessary to keep your tools in top condition.

WARNING: Always wear protective goggles when using a grindstone.

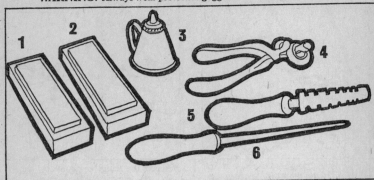

1 Tools required for sharpening are: *1.* Coarse carborundum oil stone. *2.* Fine carborundum oil stone. *3.* Oil can. *4/5.* Saw set tools. *6.* Saw file.

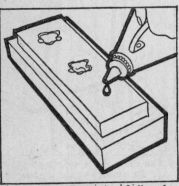

2 Apply a small quantity of oil to the carborundum stone. Do not flood it.

3 Hold chisel with bevel flat on stone at an angle of about 30°. Work back and forth. Vary tool's position on stone to save wear on it.

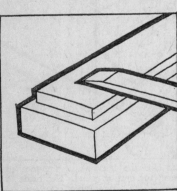

4 Draw back edge of chisel across the stone to remove any burrs.

5 To grind a chisel or plane iron edges become chipped or rounded, use a wetted sand stone with an angle guide.

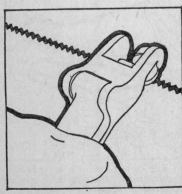

6 To use a saw set, hold saw in a vice protected by wood blocks. Set the number of teeth per inch on the dial and work along from the handle end. Clench all teeth pointing away from you. Reverse the blade and repeat.

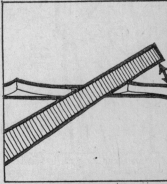

7 Now file teeth with fine triangular file. For cross cut saws the angle of file is 60°. File each alternative tooth against the front of the teeth at an angle with the line of the saw.

screws and screwdrivers

Screws are a stronger fastening than nails and have the added advantage of being retractable when required. They are also neater in appearance when properly driven in. They come in many variations classified by the type of head. Screwdrivers come in many patterns also, to meet the particular job they are designed to perform.

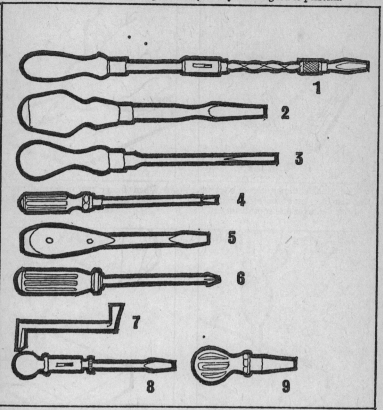

1 Various types of screwdriver: *1*. Spiral-ratchet. *2*. London. *3*. Cabinet. *4*. Electrician's. *5*. Engineer's. *6*. Pozidrive. *7*. Cranked. *8*. Ratchet. *9*. Stubby.

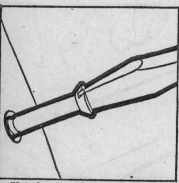

2 Use the size of screwdriver which suits the screw and the length of work. The tip should fit the screw slot.

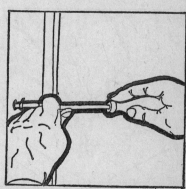

3 Always ensure that the screwdriver is held in the right manner and straight in line with the screw.

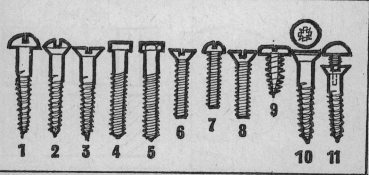

4 Various types of screw: *1*. Round head (wood). *2*. Raised head (wood). *3*. Flat head (wood). *4* and *5*. Lag screws. *6*, *7* and *8*. Metal screws. *9*. Self-Tapping. *10*. Pozidrive. *11*. Dome head (fixing mirrors, etc.)

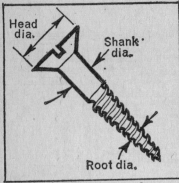

5 The principal dimensions of a screw: the diameter head for recessing, the shank diameter and root diameter.

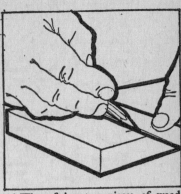

6 When fixing two pieces of wood together, mark carefully the centre lines of each hole.

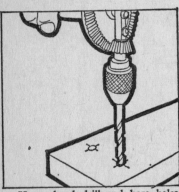

7 Use a hand drill and bore holes equal in diameter to the thickness of the screw shank. Drill as deep as the shank.

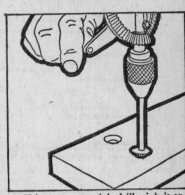

8 Using a countersink drill, sink it to the diameter of the screw head.

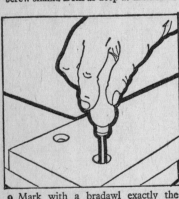

9 Mark with a bradawl exactly the centre of the holes in the wood to be joined.

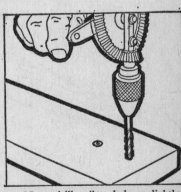

10 Now drill pilot holes, slightly smaller than the root diameter of the screw.

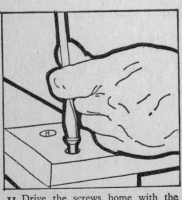

11 Drive the screws home with the screwdriver held at a vertical angle.

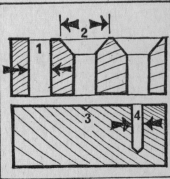

12 Complete operation: *1*. Drill the clearance hole. *2*. Countersink. *3* Obtain centre of wood to be joined. *4*. Drill pilot hole.

marking and measuring tools

Before you attempt any work you must have measuring and marking tools. These are needed in every job you do and the use of them eliminates any guess work or waste of materials.

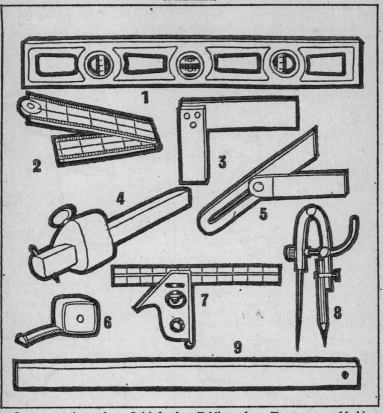

1 Some measuring tools: *1.* Spirit level. *2.* Folding rule. *3.* Try-square. *4.* Marking gauge. *5.* Bevel gauge. *6.* Metal tape measure. *7.* Combination square (level and straight) *8.* Compass. *9.* Straight edge.

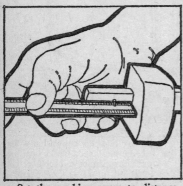

2 Set the marking gauge to distance required for transfer to work. It marks lines parallel to the planed face or edge.

3 Use of try-square: Place butt of the square against the true edge of the work and scribe the line.

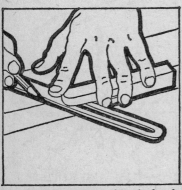

4 In a similar manner place the bevel gauge against a parallel edge of the work and obtain the desired angle.

5 Using a combination square on a rebate makes for perfect squareness.

keep your blowlamp in condition

A blowlamp, properly handled, is a safe and efficient tool for softening old paint. But it must be kept clean and be regularly checked for faults.

WARNING: Remember the heat from a blowlamp is intense. When directed on to wood and flaming paint it could cause a fire. Before leaving a job, make sure that no wood is smouldering.

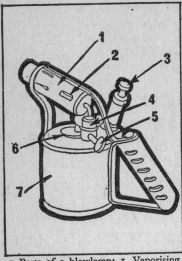

1 Parts of a blowlamp: *1.* Vaporising chamber. *2.* Nozzle aperture. *3.* Pressure pump. *4.* Filler cap. *5.* Pressure release. *6.* Spirit dish. *7.* Fuel tank.

2 Open the air vent by turning the pressure release. Light the methylated spirit. Close the vent before pumping.

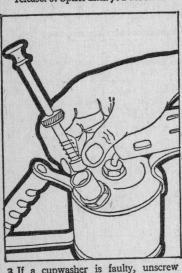

3 If a cupwasher is faulty, unscrew knurled brass cap at the top of the pump cylinder and remove plunger.

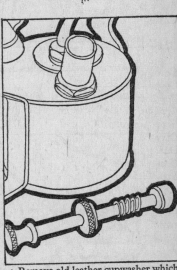

4 Remove old leather cupwasher which has become hardened. Undo retaining nut with spanner and replace.

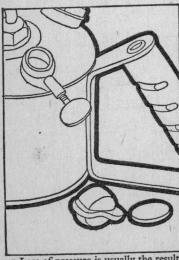

5 Loss of pressure is usually the result of a worn filler cap washer. This should be replaced.

6 For a choked nipple hole, prick with a wire pricker

types of adhesive

Each of the many branded adhesives is designed for a specific function but the handyman will probably need only four or five types, for example; Impact for laminates, PVA for wood and plastics, Expoxy resin for wood or ceramics and Latex for fabrics. A selection of some of the types on the market are shown below.

NAME	TYPE	PURPOSE
Aerolite	Resin	Wood, hardboard, laminates
Aerolite 306	Urea formaldehyde	Metal, wood, ceramics
Araldite	Expoxy resin	Metal, glass, china etc.
Bal- Tad	PVA based	Ceramic tiles
Bostick 1 clear	Rubber resin	Fabrics, wood, glass, leather etc.
Bostick contact	Synthetic rubber resin	Plastics, hardboards, rubber, laminates
Clam 2	Rubber latex	Expanded polystyrene
Clam 3	Spirit based	Melamine sheet to wood, metal, leather
Clam 7	PVA	Cement, plaster, wood, cork etc.
Cascamite	Urea formaldehyde	Wood, hardboard, laminates
Copybind	Latex china clay	Binding, carpets, rugs etc.
Copydex	Rubber latex	All fabrics, leather etc.
Croid 847	PVA (viscous)	Expanded polystyrene
Croid universal	Animal	General purpose household
Durofix	Cellulose acetate	Pottery, glass, wood plastics
Duroglue	Animal	Wood, leather, paper
Evo-stick clear	MEK acetone	Wood, china, plastics etc.
Evo-stick impact	Synthetic rubber	Plastic laminate, rubber, board etc.
Evo-stick resin	Synthetic resin	Wood
Evo-stick timme-bond	Thixotropic	Laminate sheet (adjustable bond)
Humbrol contact	Rubberised	Wood, glass, rubber, metal
Humbrol universal	PVA	Almost anything
Isobond	Polymer synthetic	Vinyls, lino, expanded polystyrene
Laybond binding	Resin latex	Joining carpets, woven fabric etc.
Nic-o-bond tile	Synthetic resin	Ceramics, expanded polystyrene
Nic-o-bond MP	PVA	Multi-purpose
Plycostic	Synthetic resin	Cork to concrete, wood etc.
Polyfix	Filled cellulose	Ceramic tiles
Tretoband universal	Water based synthetic PVA resin	Interior woodwork, leather, fabrics
Uhu all purpose	Synthetic resin	Almost anything
Uhu plus	Synthetic resin	Almost anything

Painting
and
Decorating

wall tiling

Tiles for the walls of bathrooms and kitchens now come in many beautiful patterns. Improved adhesives have helped to simplify the hanging of tiles. With care and a certain amount of skill you can make a very professional job.

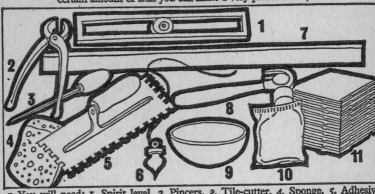

1 You will need: 1. Spirit level. 2. Pincers. 3. Tile-cutter. 4. Sponge. 5. Adhesive spreader. 6. Plumb line. 7. Wood lath. 8. Hammer. 9. Mixing bowl. 10. Adhesive. 11. Tiles. Not shown: Grouting powder.

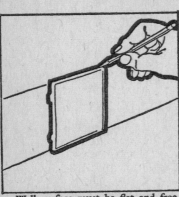

2 Wall surface must be flat and free from grease. Measure one tile up from the lowest part of the floor or skirting board.

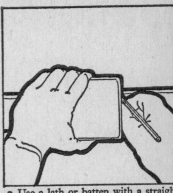

3 Use a lath or batten with a straight edge. Pencil off the tile units (including any spacer lugs).

4 Using spirit level nail the marked lath to the wall at the marked height.

5 Decide on a convenient part to start. Plumb a vertical line and mark with pencil on the wall.

6 Spread the adhesive with a combing action. Use enough for about two tiles high.

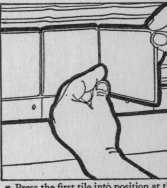

7 Press the first tile into position at the horizontal and vertical intersection. Continue with each tile.

32

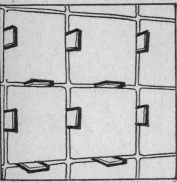

8 Built in spacer lugs keep tiles even. If no spacer lugs are available, insert pieces of card between each tile.

9 Part of a tile for corners can be cut by scoring the glazed surface with a tile cutter.

10 Place a matchstick or nail under scored line. Press the edges down firmly. The tile will now snap cleanly in two.

11 To tile round pipes or other projections, nibble out the shape with a pair of pliers.

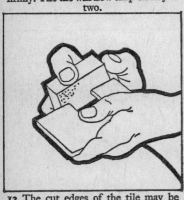

12 The cut edges of the tile may be rough. Smooth these off with a sand stone.

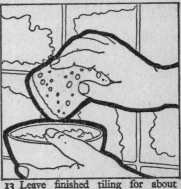

13 Leave finished tiling for about twelve hours. Then mix grout, rub well into the joints and press the solution between tiles with a rounded stick.

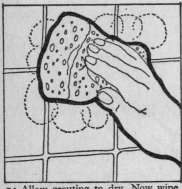

14 Allow grouting to dry. Now wipe off the surplus with a wet sponge.

15 To fix tiles around a kitchen sink unit, nail the horizontal lath above the sink to support the tiles.

repairing a hole in a plaster ceiling

In older houses lath and plaster ceilings can crack and even come away in lumps leaving a nasty hole and plenty of debris. Often the laths crack with it and the problem is to do a matching repair, providing of course that the hole is not too large.

1 A small portion of ceiling has fallen leaving an unsightly hole with broken laths.

2 Carefully peel back the surrounding ceiling paper. Generally clean up all round.

3 With a sharp knife cut away loose cracked pieces of plaster until you come to the firm plaster.

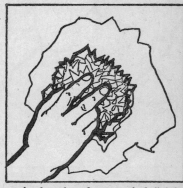

4 Apply a plug of paper soaked slightly in water.

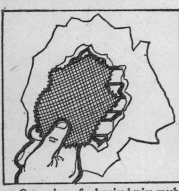

5 Cut a piece of galvanised wire mesh to size and try it to the hole for keying into the plaster.

6 Damp all around the hole in preparation for plastering.

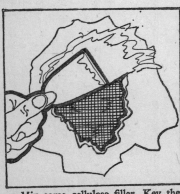

7 Mix some cellulose filler. Key the mesh into the hole and spread the filler smoothly over the whole surface.

8 Allow the filler to dry out. Sandpaper smooth. Re-decorate your ceiling.

fixing a cove to your ceiling

Coving can set off the sharpness of your room with a classical curvature and will certainly improve its appearance. It is easy to put up and inexpensive to buy. It can suit any type of room and comes in various lengths. We show here a plastic type of coving which is also fireproof.

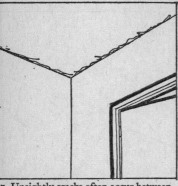

1 Unsightly cracks often occur between wall and ceiling due to movement or settlement of the house.

2 Measure and mark guide lines with a pencil along the walls and ceiling to the width of the coving.

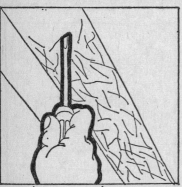

3 Scratch the surface with a sharp knife between the guide lines to provide a grip for the adhesive.

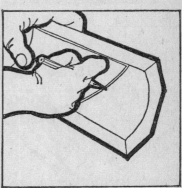

4 Measure the ceiling for length and with a paper template angled at 45°, saw a mitre with a fine toothed saw.

5 Start mixing the adhesive to the recommended consistency. Stir well.

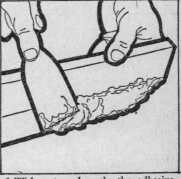

6 With a trowel apply the adhesive generously and with help push the cove into position.

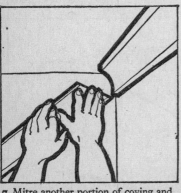

7 Mitre another portion of coving and butt up. Make good the mitres and joints with surplus adhesive. Use a springy knife to spread adhesive at the mitres.

8 Remove all traces of surplus adhesive round the coving with a wet brush. Allow to dry. It is now ready for painting.

ceiling tiles

Ceiling tiles give a smart look to ceilings and are cheap and easy to use. There are fibreboard (acoustic) tiles and expanded polystyrene tiles. Both have good thermal insulation properties. Use a recommended adhesive for both. Always work with clean hands, as every mark shows. Spread adhesive all over polystyrene tiles.

WARNING: NEVER USE OIL-BASED PAINT ON THE TILES BECAUSE OF FIRE RISK. You can use emulsion type flame-retarding paint, however. NEVER FIX TILES OVER COOKERS because of the danger of fat or cooking oil catching alight.

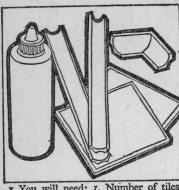

1 You will need: *1*. Number of tiles required. *2*. Adhesive. *3*. Straight edge. *4*. Sharp knife. *5*. Tape measure.

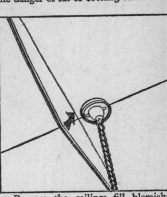

2 Prepare the ceiling; fill blemishes and clean off old distemper and grease. Measure centre of room and divide into quarters.

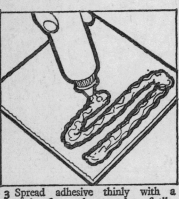

3 Spread adhesive thinly with a spreader from edge to edge of tile. Work cleanly and not over the edge.

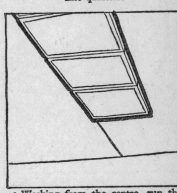

4 Working from the centre, run the tiles down the first quarter of the room.

5 Use a piece of wood or card to press tile home to prevent finger marks.

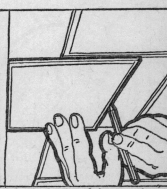

6 At the border of the room lay one tile upon the other loose one and mark a line.

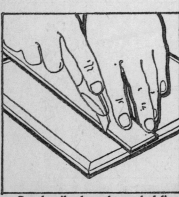

7 Cut the tile along the marked line with a sharp knife to make a border tile. Stick both into position.

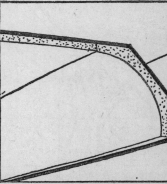

8 You can have a cornice tile in the same material to give a rounded appearance to the plain edges of the room.

painting

Painting is one of the easiest inside decorating jobs, especially with the new durable and non-drip paints. Successful painting depends on preparation and patience.

You will need: *1*. Paint stripper. *2*. Shavehooks. *3*. Blowlamp. *4*. Putty knife. *5*. Paint kettle. *6*. Sandpaper block. *7*. Wire brush. *8*. Stripping knife. Not shown: Sponge, Glass paper, Emery paper, Shellac, Cellulose filler, Paint, White spirit, Linseed oil.

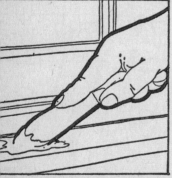

Start by filling and making good any indents or cracks in the woodwork.

3 For cracks around window joints use a good cellulose filler or stopping.

Leave filler to set then sandpaper smooth. For best results, wrap sandpaper round a block of wood.

5 Key back and thoroughly wet large holes in plaster walls.

6 Mix the required amount of filler. Trowel into the hole until it is flush with the wall.

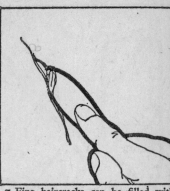

7 Fine haircracks can be filled with filler using a small flat knife or even your fingers.

8 Strip paint which is badly blistered or flaked. Use a blowlamp and shavehook in small mouldings.

9 Use a stripping knife on larger areas such as door panels. Hold the blade nearly vertical otherwise you will dig into the wood.

10 Prime all new woodwork first. Give a good coating of shellac with a brush to prevent knots from grinning through the paint.

11 Brush with a wire brush all iron work to be painted.

12 Window stays need a good brushing.

13 Now wash all surfaces with warm water. Rub down with a fine glass paper.

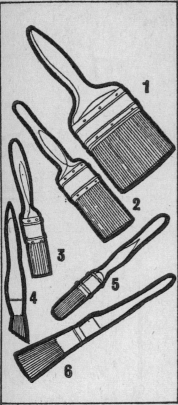

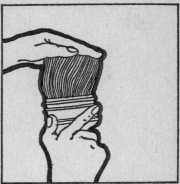

15 New brush bristles should be springy and keep their shape. Bend bristles back and forth to remove any loose hairs.

14 Brushes: *1*. Flat distemper. *2*. 2 in. flat sash. *3*. 1 in. *4*. Cutting in. *5*. Small for intricate work. *6*. Sash for rounded objects.

16 After painting with oil-based paint soak the brush in white spirit. After using emulsion paint, clean the brush in water.

17 Wash the bristles of a new brush in soapy water, moving the hairs vigorously with your fingers.

18 Rinse the brush under the cold tap.

19 Squeeze the bristles dry using an absorbent paper.

20 Dip the tip of a new brush in linseed oil to smooth the bristles to a good shape, and leave overnight. Next day, wipe bristles and dip tip of brush in white spirit before you commence painting.

21 Lever open the lid of the paint tin in several places round the lid using a coin or screwdriver to prevent damage to the rim.

22 Stir the paint well with a wooden stick to an even, smooth consistency.

23 If there are lumps or other impurities in the paint, strain it into a paint kettle through a piece of muslin or an old nylon stocking.

24 When you have finished painting, wipe the rim of the lid clean of paint and tap home securely.

25 Turn the tin upside down. Shake well to airlock the tin and its remaining contents for storage.

26 Mark the date on the tins and store

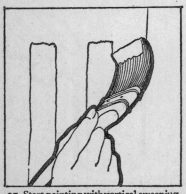

27 Start painting with vertical sweeping strokes. Cover about one-third of the brush with paint.

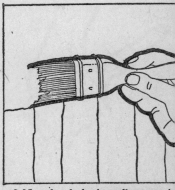

28 Now brush horizontally over the vertical strokes. Use paint sparingly.

29 Lay off vertically with less and less pressure on the bristles. Just glance the surface to eliminate brush marks.

30 Tie a thin wire across the top of the paint tin and brush off any excess paint.

31 When painting window mouldings use the lining brush which is angled for the job.

32 Use a metal or cardboard shield against the mouldings. This helps to keep the paint off the window pane.

33 Or mask the glass next to the mouldings with tape. You can then use a larger brush and paint more freely.

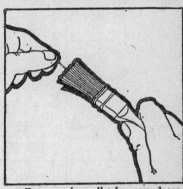

34 Remove immediately any loose hairs that appear hanging from the bristles.

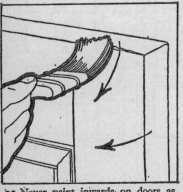

35 Never paint inwards on doors as shown here or you will build up paint on the edge and cause the door to stick.

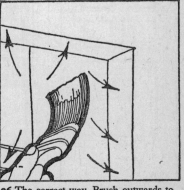

36 The correct way. Brush outwards to leave a sharp edge.

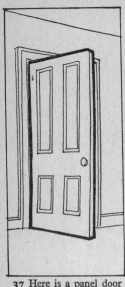

37 Here is a panel door which will be closed when painting. The sequence for painting is given as follows.

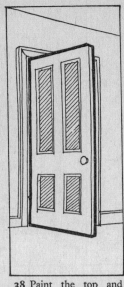

38 Paint the top and bottom panels also the moulds.

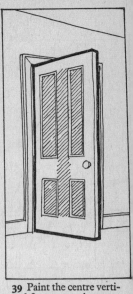

39 Paint the centre vertical from top to bottom.

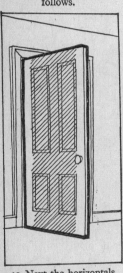

40 Next the horizontals. Begin at the top, the centre and the bottom.

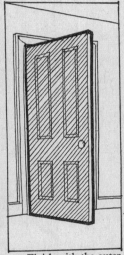

41 Finish with the outer verticals and sides of the door. Check for any paint runs with a dry brush.

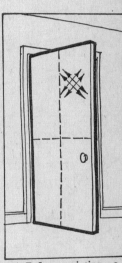

42 Before painting a flush door, divide it in quarters and paint a section at a time, finishing at the centre.

43 To paint a sash window. Push the bottom frame up to the top.

44 Lower the top frame and paint about a third of it using a ½ in. brush. If not using a guard always wipe off excess paint from glass.

45 Drop the bottom frame. Push back the top frame and finish painting.

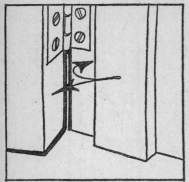

46 Reverting to doors. Do not clog the edge of the door or the surround.

47 Paint pads can be added to your range of painting tools to use instead of brushes.

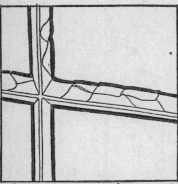

48 Exterior decorating. Sun, frost and rain deteriorate paintwork. This is an example of brittle putty.

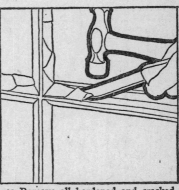

49 Remove all hardened and cracked putty carefully with a hacking knife. Tap it with care away from the glass.

50 Press in new putty. Paint the frame and allow paint to overlap on to the glass about 1/8 in. to provide a waterproof seal to the putty.

51 Use a calking gun to weather proof cracks around window frames.

52 This defect is often caused by bad quality priming, or painting over a damp surface causing the paint to flake.

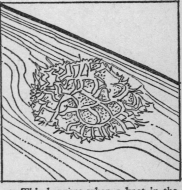

53 This happens when a knot in the wood has not been treated with knotting solution but painted over.

54 Blistering – usually the presence of moisture in paint or resin in the timber. Remove all defective paint and wait for a dry surface.

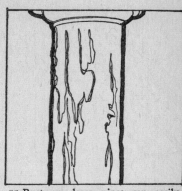

55 Rust on down pipes can easily spread even under paintwork and will eventually split the pipe.

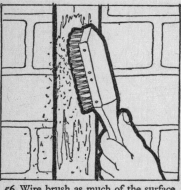

56 Wire brush as much of the surface as possible. Then emery paper down.

57 Or use your power drill with a wire brush attachment

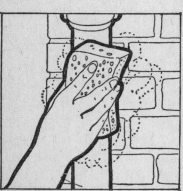

58 Wash down with hot soapy water and allow to dry.

59 Place a piece of cardboard behind the pipe to protect the brickwork. Apply grey metallic primer. Allow to dry. Paint over with gloss paint.

60 To paint gutters: scoop out all dirt and dust from the gutter. Wirebrush all the inside and outside.

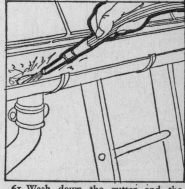

61 Wash down the gutter and the down pipe. Get rid of any deposits of particles that cause rust.

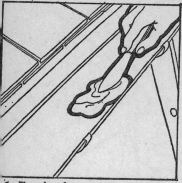

62 Examine the gutter for leaks. Patch any with a bitumastic cement. Trowel this on generously.

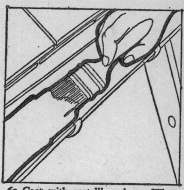

63 Coat with metallic primer. When dry apply gloss paint to the outside and paint the inside with a waterproof bitumastic paint.

64 Some of the tools required for painting the outside of the house: 1. Buckets. 2. Paint roller. 3. Brushes, 4. Wire brush. 5. Hawk. 6. Steps. 7. Sponge. 8. Trowel. 9. Ladders.

65 Outside walls: Brush away loose matter. Fill cracks. Wash down with stabilising solution. With 4 in. brush apply smooth first coat of paint.

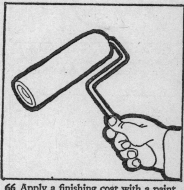

66 Apply a finishing coat with a paint roller to produce a fine textured appearance.

67 Treat absorbent surfaces such as bricks with a stabilising solution. This helps the paint to flow.

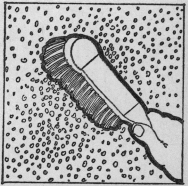

68 On rough cast surfaces apply the paint with a soft banister brush.

69 With a roller and emulsion paint you can decorate quickly and effectively. Pour a suitable amount of paint into the tray.

70 Move the roller up and down in the tray to collect the paint. Don't overload the roller.

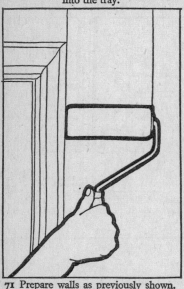

71 Prepare walls as previously shown. Apply paint with roller. This is how to cut into a door frame with the roller.

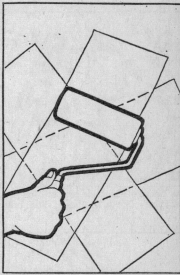

72 When painting a large surface, move the roller criss cross. The paint will dry flat and no marks will show.

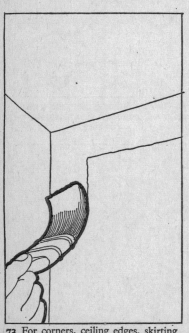

73 For corners, ceiling edges, skirting boards and window sills, use a brush.

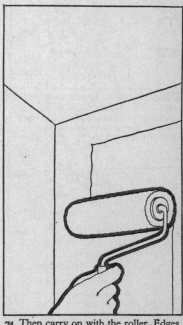

74 Then carry on with the roller. Edges can be easily damaged by the roller and it is difficult to butt into corners and edges.

PAINT FAULTS: CAUSES AND REMEDIES

FAULT	CAUSES	REMEDY
GRITTINESS	Application of paint stored for for a long while – broken paint skins.	Glass paper the surface smooth when it is dry and repaint.
BLEEDING	Discolouration —— an underlying colour or stain shows through the new paint.	Complete removal of the old affected paint; seal with aluminium paint.
BLISTERING	Blisters are caused through damp beneath the surface, or painting in a moist atmosphere.	Remove all defective paint, allow to dry and prime before applying new coat.
BLOOMING	Whitish appearance on varnishing and enamel paint because of application in moist conditions.	Bloom can be removed by rubbing the surface with a mixture of linseed oil and acetic acid. If this does not work flatten out the work and recoat.
MISSING	This occurs when a varnish or enamel paint is applied to an undercoat which has hardened.	Wash off the newly applied coat with white spirit, allow to dry and flat down with waterproof abrasive paper. Then repaint.
CRAZING	Crazing will occur when hard-drying coats of paint are applied too quickly on top of each other.	A good rubbing down over the affected part may be sufficient, then a repaint. Or remove all paint and allow adequate drying times between each painting.
CURTAINING	Usually occurs in enamel paint due to wrong brushing techniques; the film of paint tends to sag in unsightly runs.	Rub down well and give a final coat, brushing out well.
FLAKING	Moisture present beneath the surface before painting, or dampness during painting.	Remove all the paint completely, wash down and then repaint.
THINNING	Paint is of too thin a consistency and too great a contrast to the undercoat.	Always use the recommended undercoat and do not over-thin the finishing coat.
SLOW DRYING	The application of paint in damp conditions on a surface where traces of oil or grease remain.	Remove all grease or oil from the surface and start again.
SPECKS	The surface was not properly prepared or old paint containing dirt or grit has been used.	Rub down surface of the paint with abrasive paper and repaint with new stock.
WRINKLING	Occurs mostly with varnishes or enamel paints when applied too thickly. The surface becomes dry but remains soft underneath.	Strip off the affected paint and repaint allowing ample drying times.

easy paperhanging

Successful paperhanging can confidently be done by everyone. Just remember a few simple rules and don't panic. You're far more likely to have a disaster if you're too tentative. Preparation of the walls prior to wallpapering is very important and if you follow the advice given here you shouldn't have any trouble.

1 You will need: *1.* Hanging brush. *2.* Steel straight edge. *3.* Scissors. *4.* Knife. *5.* Paste brush. *6.* Seam roller. *7.* Pencil. *8.* Paper stripper. *9.* Sandpaper. *10.* Sponge. *11.* Steps. *12.* Paste bucket. *13.* Folding ruler. *14.* Chalk. *15.* Plumb bob. *16.* Pasting table. Not shown: Crack filler, Glue size, Paste, Chemical remover.

2 Mix some chemical remover in warm water. Give the old paper two soakings with a sponge.

3 Strip the old paper a section at a time with a stripping knife. Collect the strippings in old newspaper as you go along to save mess.

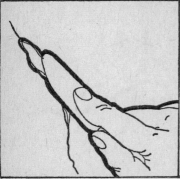

4 When all the old paper is off, fill any hair cracks in the wall with a proprietory filler.

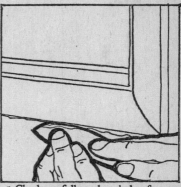

5 Check carefully under window frames where cracks can occur. Fill any that you find.

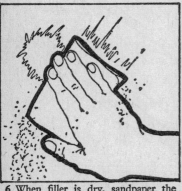

6 When filler is dry, sandpaper the walls to remove blemishes and pieces of old wallpaper that may be left behind.

7 Mix some glue size in a bucket. Apply to the walls with a brush to reduce poracity and to help the new paper to slide during hanging.

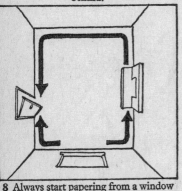

8 Always start papering from a window and work round from both sides towards the door.

9 Prepare the wallpaper paste in a bucket, stir well and leave until it becomes firm, usually fifteen minutes.

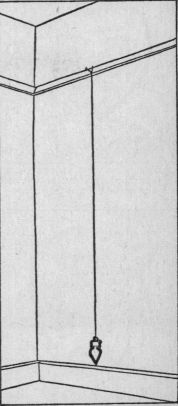

10 Measure the width of your wallpaper. Transfer this measurement to the wall. Hang a plumbline for your guidance.

11 Chalk the string. Now hold the plumb bob still against the wall, pluck the string and let snap back to leave a vertical chalk line.

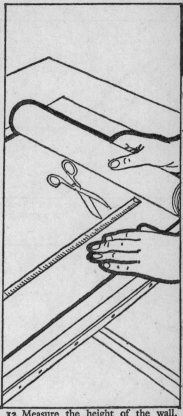

12 Measure the height of the wall. This is the length of your first sheet, plus 4 in. surplus. Mark the measurement with a pencil.

13 Draw a line across. Using a straight edge tear the paper across, or cut across your marked line with the scissors.

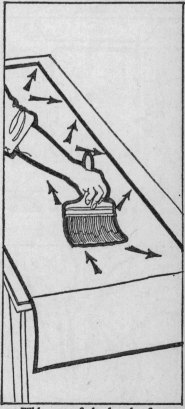

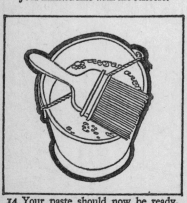

14 Your paste should now be ready. Tie a cord across the paste bucket which will act as a brush rest.

15 With part of the length of your paper on the table, paste from the centre outwards.

16 Be generous with the paste and make sure that the sides of the paper have enough paste. This is important.

17 When this half has been pasted take the top of the paper and fold it to the centre. Move this pasted fold along and paste the other half.

18 Now fold the bottom of the paper to the centre. Carry folded paper over your arm to steps placed where you are going to hang.

19 Take the top edge in both hands, paste side towards the wall. Allow 2 in. overlap at the top. Unfold the paper.

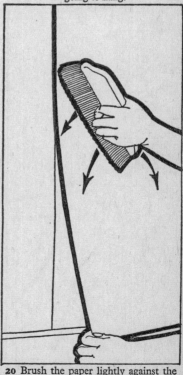

20 Brush the paper lightly against the wall following your chalk line down to the skirting board.

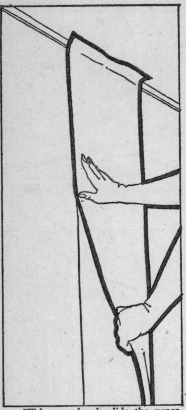

21 With your hands slide the paper exactly to the chalk line. Don't be afraid to lift the paper from the wall and begin again.

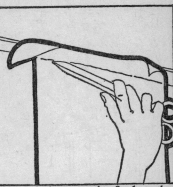

22 Brush the top section firmly to the ceiling edge or picture rail. Score a line at the bottom edge with the back edge of scissors.

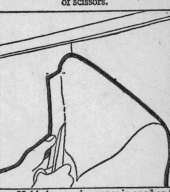

23 Hold the surplus paper in one hand and peel back enough to cut along the crease you have made. Brush the paper firmly back.

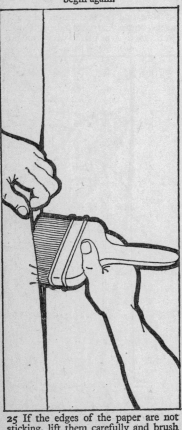

25 If the edges of the paper are not sticking, lift them carefully and brush paste down behind the edge.

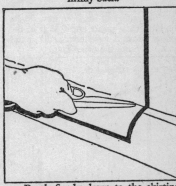

24 Brush firmly down to the skirting board, smoothing out any bubbles as you go. Score a line along the skirting and cut off surplus paper.

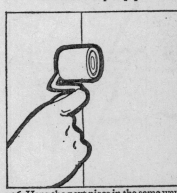

26 Hang the next piece in the same way, butting it to the first piece. You will find a seam roller useful to lock the butt joint.

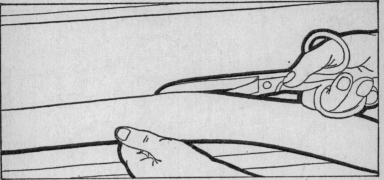

27 For odd widths round windows and doors, measure the width required and cut to length allowing ½ in. waste.

28 Fit the strip into the window, butting carefully. Cut off surplus paper.

29 If a window frame juts into the width of a piece, cut to length and hang. Brush well into window frame. Score round frame and cut off surplus.

30 Here the paper passes over the window ledge. Cut to fit and trim away surplus.

31 When a piece of paper butts up with the waste under the window ledge brush well under the ledge and trim.

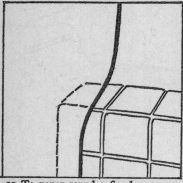

32 To paper round a fireplace, press the paper against the edges to get a line of the shape.

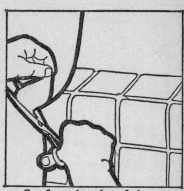

33 Cut from the edge of the paper diagonally up to the marks.

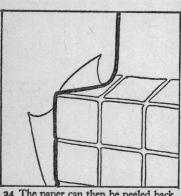

34 The paper can then be peeled back and the surplus cut away. Smooth the paper into place over the fireplace.

35 To paper into more difficult shapes, use the same procedure but you will need more cuts so that the paper can follow the contours.

36 To paper round a circular switch, pierce a hole and let the switch burst through. Make star cuts, press paper into position. Trim.

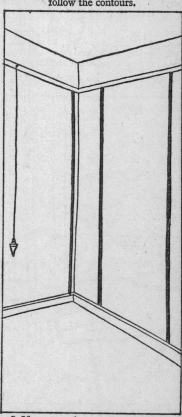

37 Do the same for flush mounted switches but use a sharp knife. If cover plate is removed for a neater job, SWITCH OFF ELECTRICITY SUPPLY.

38 If you reach a corner and only a small piece of paper is needed, measure and cut with extra $\frac{1}{2}$ in. for corner turn. Plumb for next length.

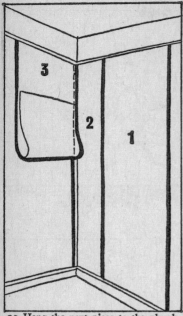

39 Hang the next piece to the plumb line, pasting over the $\frac{1}{2}$ in. overlap. If paper is patterned, make sure the pattern matches here.

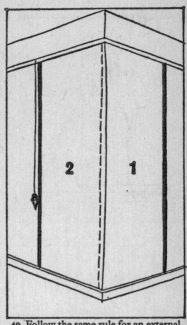

40 Follow the same rule for an external corner. Cut the paper to allow for an inch round the corner. The next piece plumbed and matched.

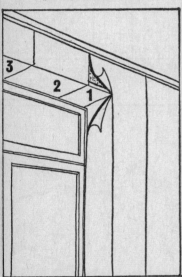

41 To paper into a bay window, use small fillets *1, 2, 3* as shown with 1 in. overlap. Then paste the full piece over them.

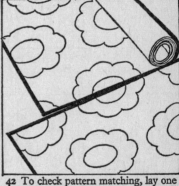

42 To check pattern matching, lay one piece next to another. Move along until you find the match. You will get some waste with most patterns.

43 This matches and is called a set pattern. All lengths can be identical.

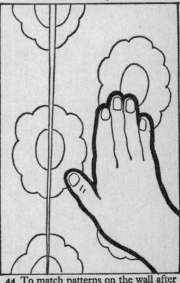

44 To match patterns on the wall after pasting. Push the paper with your hand. This will stretch it and match correctly.

45 If you get a blister in the paper when it is pasted, make a sharp incision across the blister with a razor blade.

46 Pull back each segment carefully and paste each one.

47 Brush back lightly into place, and you won't notice it.

48 For torn wallpaper, tear off the damaged area.

49 Cut and match a similar piece of paper, slightly larger than the damaged area.

50 Tear or scallop a ragged edge round the piece of matching paper.

51 Paste and match the edges of the patch. Brush back carefully into place.

52 To remove grease or finger marks, use a warm iron and blotting paper.

53 To paper a ceiling, use a scaffold board supported by a sturdy pair of steps and a strong box.

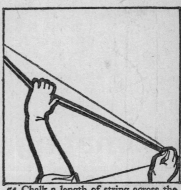

54 Chalk a length of string across the length of the room starting parallel with the main window.

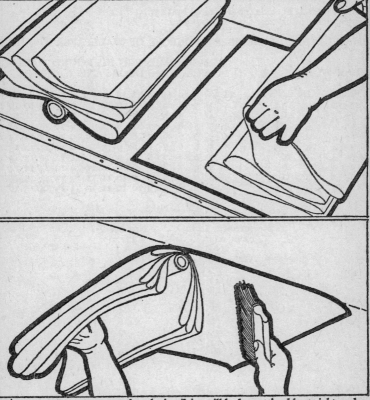

55 Paper may be run across or lengthwise. Joins will be less noticeable at right angles to the main window. Ceiling paper will be much longer than wallpaper so paste in sections and fold. Balance folded paper on a spare roll of paper. Position against chalk line. Brush first section and open next, repeating as you go along.

56 To cut round a light rose, pierce the paper and make a series of star cuts.

57 Score the outline of the rose on the paper with the back of scissors and cut off surplus paper.

estimating wallpaper

To estimate the amount of paper needed to cover the walls of a room, measure the length and width of the room, including door space and windows. Then measure the height of the room from skirting board to ceiling (or picture rail). Compare these measurements with the wall-chart below and read off the number of rolls required. Use the room measurements also for the ceiling paper chart.

English wallpaper is 21 in. wide (after trimming) by 12 yd. Rolls of paper are supplied in batches each with a serial number. Take a note of the number in case you need to re-order.

Lining paper: 22 in. wide (no trimming) by 12 yd.

Border paper and friezes: 1 roll is about 9 yd.

CALCULATION OF NUMBER OF PIECES OF WALLPAPER REQUIRED

HEIGHT IN FT. FROM SKIRTING			28	32	36	40	44	48	52	56	60	64	68	72	76	80	84	88
7	and under	7½	4	4	5	5	6	6	7	7	8	8	9	9	9	10	10	11
7½	,,	8	4	4	5	5	6	6	7	8	8	9	9	10	10	11	11	12
8	,,	8½	4	5	5	6	6	7	7	8	8	9	9	10	10	11	12	13
8½	,,	9	4	5	5	6	6	7	8	8	9	9	10	11	11	12	12	13
9	,,	9½	4	5	6	6	7	7	8	9	9	10	10	11	12	12	13	13
9½	,,	10	5	5	6	7	7	8	9	9	10	10	11	12	12	13	14	14
10	,,	10½	5	5	6	7	8	8	9	10	10	11	12	12	13	14	14	15
10½	,,	11	5	6	7	7	8	9	9	10	11	11	12	13	13	14	15	16
11	,,	11½	5	6	7	8	8	9	10	10	11	12	13	13	14	15	16	16

CEILINGS

Measurement in ft. round room	Number of Pieces
20 – 28	1
30 – 40	2
42 – 48	3
52 – 58	4
60 – 66	5
68 – 70	6
74 – 78	7
80 – 82	8
86 – 88	9
90 – 92	10

Doors and Windows

fitting a hinge

At some time you may have to fit or adjust a hinge. There are many types of hinges but here we show how to fit a butt hinge, the most common type.

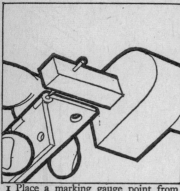

1 Place a marking gauge point from the centre of the hinge and the hinge end tight against the head of the gauge, and mark off as at 1. (illustration 3).

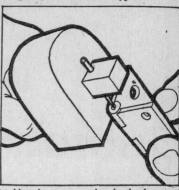

2 Alter the gauge to give depth of recess with the head of the gauge to the centre of the hinge pin. Mark off as at 2. (illustration 3).

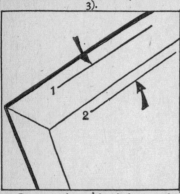

3 Gauge marks on the timber to take the hinge. Only scribe approximate length of hinge – scribe marks are unsightly.

4 Mark off exactly the length of hinge with a try square in the position you are going to fit it.

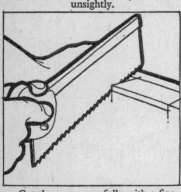

5 Cut the recess carefully with a fine-tooth tenon. Chisel out to the back line the waste wood.

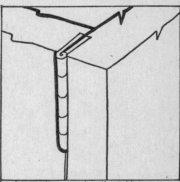

6 Fit hinge with 2 screws. Place against flap to be hinged. Mark round the hinge flap. To recess this flap cut as previous. The hinges should be screwed and the flap tested for minor adjustments.

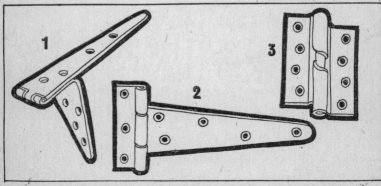

7 Other types of hinges: 1. Box hinge: useful on thin plywood doors or boxes. 2. Tee hinge used for ledged doors. Two are used. 3. Rising butt allowing the door to rise above carpet or uneven floor.

curing a sticking door

There may be several reasons why a door sticks or rattles. Here are some remedies for some faults. Remember when using a plane that what you take off cannot be replaced very easily.

1 You will need: *1.* Wood plugs. *2.* Screwdriver. *3.* Hammer. *4.* Plane.

2 Heavy overpainting on edges and rebate can cause sticking, more so if hinges are painted. Sandpaper down.

3 Check for all loose screws in the hinges. Remove the screws if they won't hold.

4 Place a wedge under door for support. Tap suitable size wood plugs into holes and re-screw. For large holes apply wood filler and longer screws.

5 If door binds at bottom apply coarse abrasive paper underneath and swing the door across it a few times.

6 If door still binds, replace wedge, unscrew hinge, put a shim of cardboard at back of hinge, replace flap and rescrew.

7 Should door bind at the top, find where a high spot shows and plane off excess wood. Sandpaper smooth.

8 Lubricate each hinge, but not if they are nylon.

flush panelling a door

Transform an old-fashioned panelled door into a smart flush door with the latest tempered hardboard panels. Plane and scrape any high spots on an old door which might prevent the hardboard panel from bedding flat. Damp the reverse side when cutting your hardboard and allow to cure in room temperature for about 48 hours.

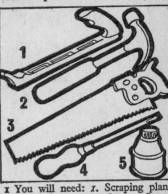

1 You will need: *1.* Scraping plane *2.* Light hammer. *3.* Saw *4.* Screwdriver. *5.* Impact adhesive.

2 Make sure that the door is hanging well and the hinges are in good order. See that the lock is working satisfactorily.

3 Remove all the door furniture handles, lock and finger plate.

4 Take the door off by unscrewing the hinges. Get someone to hold the door while you do this.

5 Place it horizontally on stout supports. Wood pack and glue recessed panels flush with door edges. Plane down protruding mouldings if not flush.

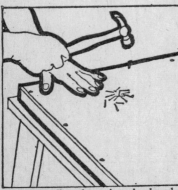

6 Cut hardboard to size. Apply adhesive and panel pin round the edges at intervals. Recess pins. Fill with wood filler. Find and drill hole for handle.

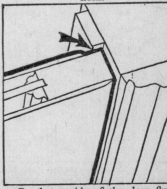

7 Panel one side of the door flush. Make allowance for closing on the rebate side as shown above.

62

fixing a new letter box

If, after painting your front door, the old letter box looks out of place, you may want to replace it with a new one. This is quite a simple job and with a few tools should only take a couple of hours.

1 The old letter box is worn, the spring does not work and the slit is too small for some letters. Remove it.

2 Buy new box to size. Measure size of flap and mark on door. Drill holes in each corner. Be careful to drill same bottom angle as old aperture.

3 With a padsaw, cut from the holes to the old aperture keeping the slope the same at the bottom.

4 Carefully chisel out any uneven or ragged edges of the new aperture.

5 Sandpaper the whole opening to a smooth finish.

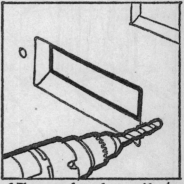

6 Place new letter box outside the door. Mark the new hole centre. Drill the holes, keeping the drill straight.

7 Place letter box to door with bolts through. Most of them have a side adjustment bar which helps to keep the letter box aligned.

8 Tighten the two nuts on to the washers and try the flap. You may have to chamfer a little in places if tight.

repair to a doorpost

Exposed softwood doorpost surrounds usually suffer from the weather. Wet rot can occur at the base of the door frame after constant splashing from rainwater. Ruthless action is needed – cut out the rotten wood and replace it with new.

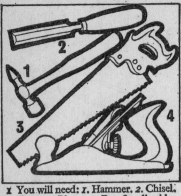

1 You will need: *1*. Hammer. *2*. Chisel. *3*. Saw. *4*. Plane. *5*. Proofing liquid – preservative.

2 This is the area where the post is liable to rot.

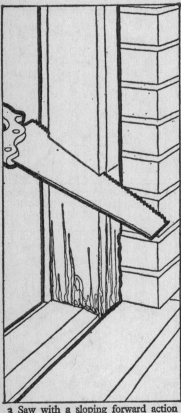

3 Saw with a sloping forward action at about 45° an inch or so above the rotted wood. The door stop is also sawn.

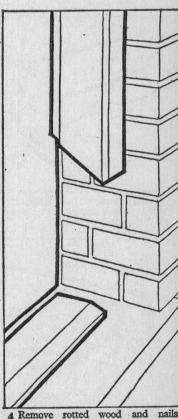

4 Remove rotted wood and nails that have held it to the wall. Clean up wall surface with stiff brush and fill any crevices.

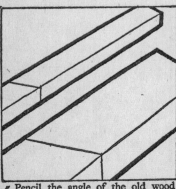

5 Pencil the angle of the old wood on to the new wood and cut the same angle slightly oversize. Now plane smooth down to size.

6 Coat both pieces of new wood with wood preservative especially the end grains. Fix back with masonry nails. Prime and repaint the new wood.

erecting a space saving door

Doors take up a lot of space because you have to keep furniture and cabinets clear of them. Small kitchens suffer by losing a great deal of their floor space. By taking down the door and adding a sliding space saving door you will gain valuable space. This type folds neatly back into concertina pleats when closed.

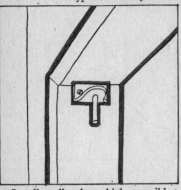

1 Install a wall anchor as high as possible in the centre of the door jamb on the side where back flap of door will be fastened.

2 Centre the track which must fit the width of the door opening. Fasten only one end with a screw so that track can swing freely.

3 Slide nylon glide wheels of panel on to the track. Re-align track and tighten remaining screws to hold door in place. Attach door panels to wall anchor.

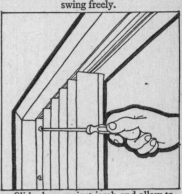

4 Slide door against jamb and allow to hang freely. Hold anchor flap against jamb and mark through eyelets for screw position.

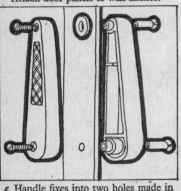

5 Handle fixes into two holes made in the leading edge to accommodate it.

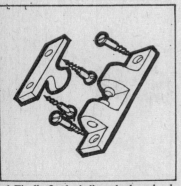

6 Finally fix the ball catch about level with the handle.

7 Standard heights of finished doors are 6 ft. 6 in., 6 ft. 8 in. and 8 ft. Widths are 2 ft. 3 in., 2 ft. 9 in. and 3 to 4 ft. up to 8 ft. Bottom clearance should be $\frac{1}{4}$ in.

how to fit a mortise lock

Fitting a mortise lock is quite a simple job provided you work accurately and make it a good fit.

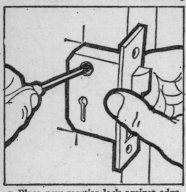

1 Place new mortise lock against edge of door. Mark position of spindle and keyhole accurately. Drill the two holes to the correct size. Pencil in length of lock.

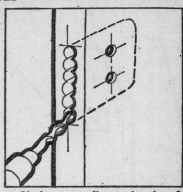

2 Obtain a centre line on the edge of the door. Pencil in the height of the lock face. Drill successive holes to the correct depth and rear width of mortise.

3 With a chisel smooth up the slot, removing the ridges left by the drill.

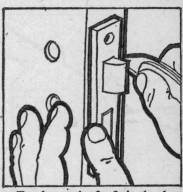

4 Try the mortise for fit in the slot. Work round the mortise face with a knife.

5 With a chisel cut out the rectangle just deep enough to take the face of the mortise lock.

6 Replace lock. Screw tightly in the recess. Check that the holes for the handle coincide. Insert knob spindle. Screw in keyhole and plate.

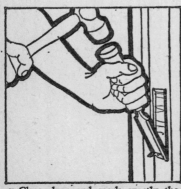

7 Close door and mark exactly the position for the striker plate on the jamb. Carefully chisel out to the depth of the plate.

8 Screw plate in position. With a chisel cut back slots to receive lock catch and bolt. Test door. Make minor adjustments if necessary.

cutting glass

Do not be frightened of cutting glass. With care and practice on small pieces of waste glass and by following the stages shown below, there is no reason why you should not cut glass to any size you require. Remember to wear protective gloves and use a cloth on sharp edges.

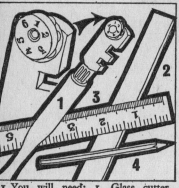

1 You will need: *1.* Glass cutter. *2.* Straight edge. *3.* Measure. *4.* Pencil crayon. Not shown: Sandstone.

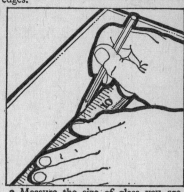

2 Measure the size of glass you are going to cut. Lay on a flat surface and mark the lines with crayon.

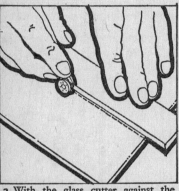

3 With the glass cutter against the straight edge, score along with even pressure running off the edge of the glass.

4 Place glass over straight edge with the score mark exactly along one edge. Press each side of the glass. It should snap cleanly in two.

5 If the glass does not snap, tap the underside gently along the score mark. Repeat with straight edge as before.

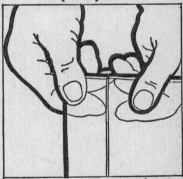

6 Small strips can be snapped by placing the index fingers close together under the glass as shown.

7 If you get a few ragged edges, use the notch of the cutter and snap downwards from the score line.

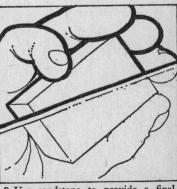

8 Use sandstone to provide a final smooth finish to the edge of the glass.

replacing a pane of glass

If you have a broken window and a builder is not available, do not just patch the broken glass with brown paper and forget it. Here's how you can tackle the job yourself. You will need a putty knife, chisel, hacking knife, pincers and hammer. Always wear gloves and beware of jagged splinters.

1 Measure width and depth of window frame. Deduct ⅛ in. from each dimension for correct size of glass. Chisel out carefully as much putty as possible.

2 Tap out with a hammer the larger sheets of glass or stick brown paper over the glass, then tap. This will stop splinters from flying.

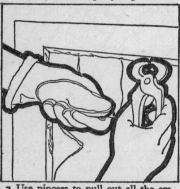

3 Use pincers to pull out all the embedded sprigs from around the frame.

4 Clear out all the remaining putty in the rebate using a hacking knife.

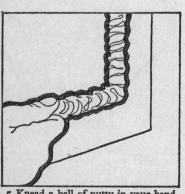

5 Knead a ball of putty in your hand and press it all round the frame into the rebate with your thumb.

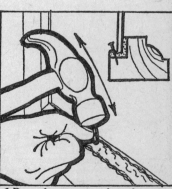

6 Press the new pane into the putty. Hammer sprigs at intervals. Let the hammer slide slowly over the pane to avoid cracking it.

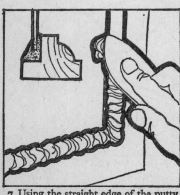

7 Using the straight edge of the putty knife, scrape off all surplus putty to give a first smoothing angle.

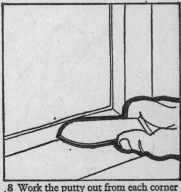

8 Work the putty out from each corner mitre so that it finishes flush with the front edge of frame. Leave to harden before painting.

fixing up a curtain rail

You can now buy some very attractive curtain rails in plastic or metal to fit all shapes and sizes of windows. They are fairly easy to instal but you will have to decide whether you want the track inside or outside the window reveal.

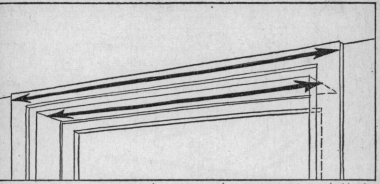

1 Once you have decided whether you want your curtains inside or outside the aperture of the window, take measurements. Decide on the drop measurement of your curtains.

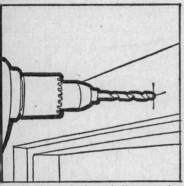

2 Obtain a horizontal line to the window architrave and drill to $\frac{1}{4}$ in. extreme holes for the maximum width with holes between spread at 1 ft. 3 in. apart to take the supports.

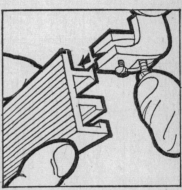

3 Slide the three or four supporting lugs along the length of top track.

4 Slide the required number of runners on the bottom track.

5 Fix the end stops at each end of the length of track to prevent the runners coming off.

6 Screw home tight each supporting lug to its respective drill hole. Get someone to hold one end of the track while you do this.

7 Hook on the curtains to each runner in turn. Don't forget to hook in to the end stop at each end of the track.

fitting a new sashcord

Sashcords wear with constant use, and can break at awkward times, but they are quite simple to replace.

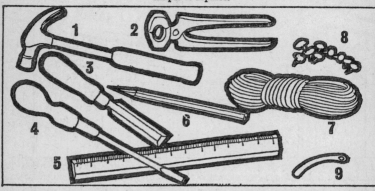

1 You will need: *1.* Hammer. *2.* Pincers. *3.* Wood chisel. *4.* Screwdriver. *5.* Ruler. *6.* Pencil. *7.* Sashcord. *8.* Clout nails. *9.* Mouse (professional term) or small weight.

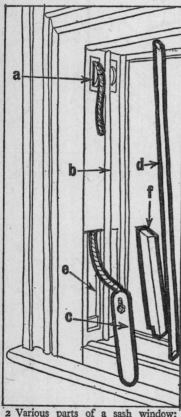

2 Various parts of a sash window: *a.* Pulley. *b.* Centrebead. *c.* Weight. *d.* Outer bead removed. *e.* Weight compartment. *f.* Pulley trap removed.

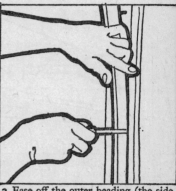

3 Ease off the outer beading (the side of the broken cord) with a chisel, using the flat side in order not to damage the wood.

4 Lift out the lower sash carefully and support one end against a chair or steps.

5 Remove the pulley trap. If this is stiff, use a screwdriver to lever it out.

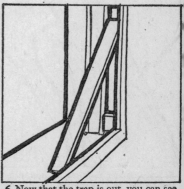

6 Now that the trap is out, you can see the weight at the bottom of the compartment.

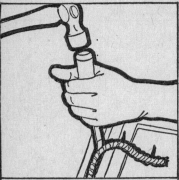

7 Remove the rotted cord from the sash groove with an old chisel.

8 Now take the weight out of the compartment and remove the old cord from the weight.

9 Tie the new sash cord with string to the 'mouse' or small weight. Feed it over the pulley into the box compartment.

10 'Mouse' will lead the sash cord to the trap.

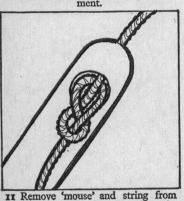

11 Remove 'mouse' and string from cord and make a good knot into the weight as shown.

12 Tie a knot in the other end of the cord, hold the lower sash to the top of the window frame and mark where pulley starts.

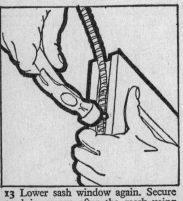

13 Lower sash window again. Secure cord in groove after the mark using clout nails – at least 3 or 4 nails. Cut rest of cord.

14 Slide window back into frame and test it. Now you can put the trap and beading back into position.

restoring a cracked window sill

Cracks appear in window sills in older houses where flaking occurs through age and in new houses where movement or settlement takes place. Sand-cement plastered in the cracks looks unsightly because the new mix often dries out a different colour. It is best to re-surface the whole top of the sill.

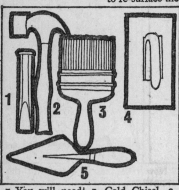

1 You will need: 1. Cold Chisel. 2. Hammer. 3. Brush. 4. Steel float. 5. Trowel. Not shown: Wooden shutter, Sand, Cement.

2 Cracks occur in many sills due to weathering or bad materials.

3 With a hammer and chisel carefully chip to a small depth along the sill. Beware of flying fragments.

4 With an old brush soak the whole surface until it is thoroughly wet.

5 Mix three parts sand and one part cement. Stir to a smooth paste and start to trowel it on.

6 Hold a wooden shutter (or batten) against the edge to help contain the wet mix.

7 Smooth up with a steel float, keeping the blade at a slight angle.

8 Remove wood shutter. Smooth front edge of the sill. Leave to set hard for two days.

fitting a louvre window

A louvre window gives you plenty of light and air and is designed to prevent draughts. Convert the old window by removing the sash frames and making good the surround. There should be a flat surface of at least 1½ in. all round to take the louvre window frame. Measure up the width and length of the window before you go to the dealer or manufacturer to purchase the louvre components – he will certainly help you.

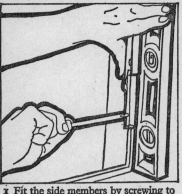

1 Fit the side members by screwing to the window surround. Use spirit level to check they are parallel and in alignment.

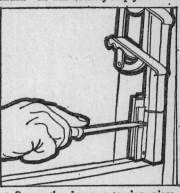

2 Screw the lower extension piece which holds the fixed pane of glass to the size you ordered.

3 Cut the weatherstrip to size for fit between the jambs. Bed this strip in mastic and screw down at intervals.

4 Fix the top strip in a similar manner. Bed also in mastic.

5 Carefully slide each glass strip between each frame and into the retaining clips. Squeeze them tight.

6 To test, place a thin piece of paper between each pane of glass and close them tight. Each pane should grip the paper.

7 Here the panes are open. Go all round and check that the clips are OK and finger tight and that all screws are home.

8 Test the operating lever from closed tight to fully open position.

Electrical
Repairs

replacing a fuse

Fuses are safety valves in a circuit. If a circuit is overloaded your fuse breaks first and protects the wiring. Always use the correct amp rating of wire or cartridge, 5, 15, or 30 amps (colour code spots: white, blue, red). If in doubt call in an electrician.

WARNING: ALWAYS SWITCH OFF THE MAIN SWITCH before removing a fuse.

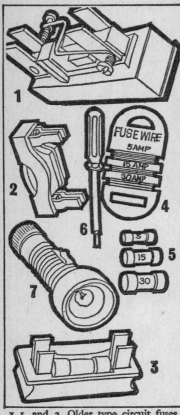

2 This is a modern fuse box. Turn off the main switch FIRST. Always carry a torch.

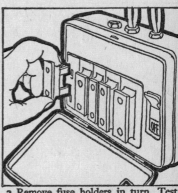

1 *1*. and *2*. Older type circuit fuses. *3*. Cartridge fuse. *4*. Fuse wire. *5*. Cartridges. *6*. Screwdriver. *7*. Torch.

3 Remove fuse holders in turn. Test cartridges in turn against metal cased torch. Figure 7 shows how to do this.

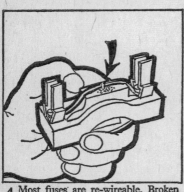

4 Most fuses are re-wireable. Broken wire and scorch marks show blown fuse.

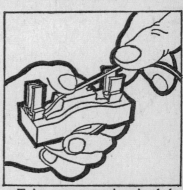

5 Twist new correct rating wire clockwise around screws. Don't strain wire by screwing too tight.

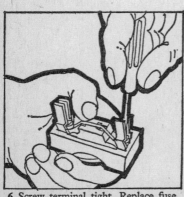

6 Screw terminal tight. Replace fuse, close box, turn on main switch. If fuse blows again your appliance could be faulty.

7 Switch on torch. Unscrew cap. Cartridge ends should touch casing and battery. Torch should light if fuse is good. Must be metal casing.

extending a flex

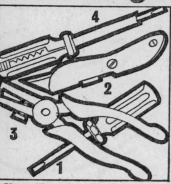

You will need: *1.* Insulated screwdriver. *2.* Strip Knife. *3.* Wire stripper. *4.* Neon tester screwdriver.

2 Cut through insulation about 2 in. from end. Take care not to damage insulation on the wires.

With wire stripper remove enough insulation around the individual wires to make the connection.

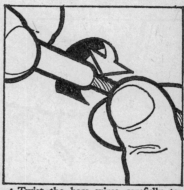

4 Twist the bare wires carefully to tighten the strands.

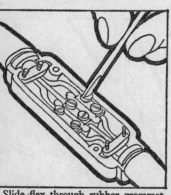

Slide flex through rubber grommet connector. Connect each wire to a terminal on one side of block. Connect wires of same colour to other side of block. Screw tight.

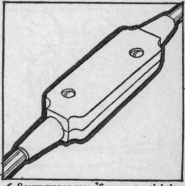

6 Screw upper case of connector tightly to lower one. The completed union makes a safe compact connection joint.

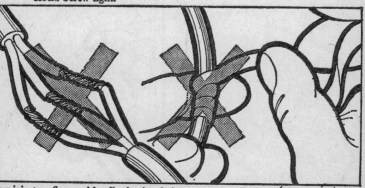

Never join two flexes with adhesive insulating tape. These joints can easily pull apart and are *highly dangerous.* Use an approved flex connector. *Always make sure the flex is not connected to a plug in a live socket.* Some houses will still have old colour coding. Here are the old codes and the corresponding new ones. OLD: Red (L) Black (N) Green (E). NEW: Brown (L) Blue (N) Green/Yellow (E).

wiring a plug

A 13-amp ring main plug has its own 13-amp fuse. Don't use a 13-amp fuse for every plug. You must find one correctly rated for your appliance. The right flex is fitted to new appliances now and watts are marked on the maker's plate to help you buy the correct fuse. NEVER USE A LARGER FUSE THAN THE ONE RECOMMENDED. Remember the colour codes. Brown (live) R.H. Terminal. Blue (neutral) L.H. Terminal. Yellow/Green (earth) Top Terminal.

1 Undo the main screw of the plug with a screwdriver.

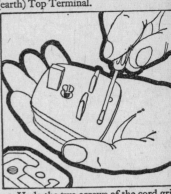

2 Undo the two screws of the cord grip plate at the base of the plug. Take off the plug cover.

3 Trim about 2 in. of outer flex. Carefully strip ½ in. off the 3 insulated cores with sharp knife. Earth wire must be long enough to reach top terminal.

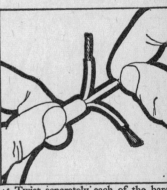

4 Twist separately each of the bare tips of the 3 wires neatly and compactly.

5 Swing aside cord grip of plug. Remove cartridge fuse and loosen the three terminal screws.

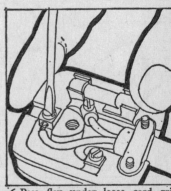

6 Pass flex under loose cord grip. Loop twisted wires round correct terminals – see colour code. Tighten screws of terminals.

7 Replace cartridge fuse and cord grip. Check correct connections. There should be no stray wires visible. Make sure you use the correct fuse. A 3-amp fuse (red) takes up to 720 watts. A 13-amp fuse (brown) takes from 720 to 3,000 watts.

8 Replace plug cover and screw the main screw tightly. Now tighten the cord grip screws.

re-wiring a
lighting point

A light flex which is brittle or worn is highly dangerous. At the first sign of wear the flex should be replaced.

WARNING: The MAIN SWITCH MUST BE TURNED OFF before commencing this job.

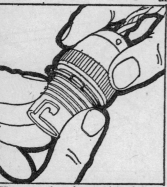

Unscrew the ring which fastens the shade to the holder. Remove the shade. Then unscrew the top off the lampholder.

2 Unscrew terminals in the top of the holder and remove flex.

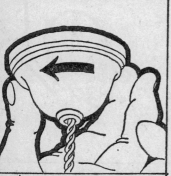

Unscrew the ceiling rose in an anticlockwise direction.

4 Loosen terminal screws. Remove old flex.

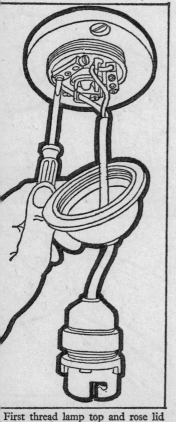

First thread lamp top and rose lid with new plastic flex. Rewire to rose and to lampholder.

6 This modern ceiling rose is designed especially for the loop-in system, but is wired similarly.

replacing an element in an electric fire

There are many different types of electric fire on the market, but they differ essentially only in design. The open type has a fine wire coiled round an element or a coiled wire encased in a block of fire clay. The enclosed type is in a silica-glass tube. Here's how to remove and replace a broken element in certain types of electric fires.

WARNING: NEVER attempt these repairs with the plug in a live socket.

1 The element wire has broken. Press the guard slightly inwards and release from casing.

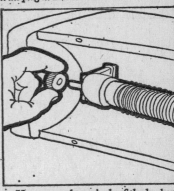

2 Unscrew end terminals of the broken element. Pull out from support brackets. Put in new one of right length and size. Screw up terminals.

3 Should your bowl fire fail to work, check if the coil has broken. If not check the flex and plug.

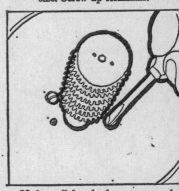

4 If the coil has broken, remove the guard from the rim. With a screwdriver remove the two element-fixing screws.

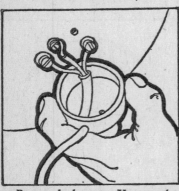

5 Remove back cover. Unscrew the two element screws. Insert new element. Tighten screws. Replace back cover.

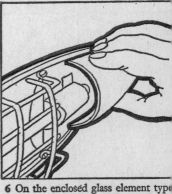

6 On the enclosed glass element type press together the two sprung on end housings. Unscrew guard and remove.

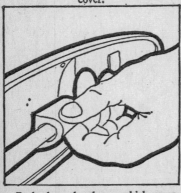

7 Push along the sleeves which cover the terminal brackets at each end.

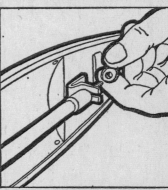

8 Unscrew the end terminal nuts. Carefully lift out the glass element and refit the new one.

repairs to an electric kettle

If your kettle fails to work, this may be due to several faults. First examine the mains' socket plug to see if it is OK. Check the wires and fuse. Check the mains' socket itself by trying another appliance in it, If these are all OK check the lead from the plug to the kettle plug. If faulty replace with new lead. If the fault is due to none of these, examine the kettle plug itself for any fault. Or it could be that the element in the kettle is faulty. This is how to replace one.

WARNING: Never carry out any repairs with the plug connected to the mains' socket.

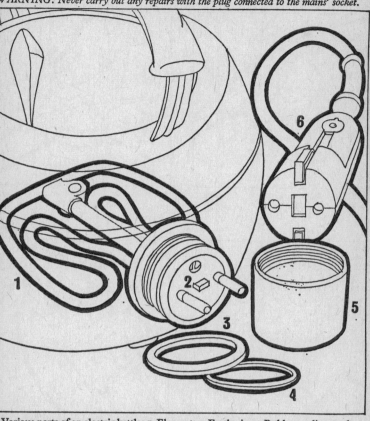

Various parts of an electric kettle: *1.* Element. *2.* Earth pin. *3.* Rubber sealing washer. *4.* Fibre washer. *5.* Kettle shroud. *6.* Kettle plug.

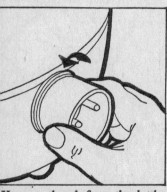

Unscrew shroud from the kettle body.

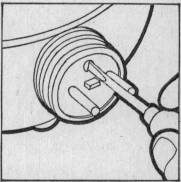

3 Unscrew two retaining screws which hold the element inside the kettle, for easy removal of element. Buy similar element from electrical shop.

Slip new sealing washer over the ead and replace in kettle. Fit the fibre sher and screw up tight the shroud. *E SURE THE ELEMENT IS NOT OUCHING THE BASE OF KETTLE.*

5 This older type kettle connector has two connecting metal clips joined to both sides, which make earth through the kettle's body.

re-wiring a modern kettle connector

This modern type of flex connector in your kettle is not as likely to need attention as the older type, but there comes a time when the flex will wear and need replacing.

WARNING: MAKE SURE THAT THE APPLIANCE IS NOT CONNECTED TO THE SOCKET.

1 Start by unscrewing the connector base screw.

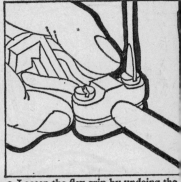

2 Loosen the flex grip by undoing the screws slightly.

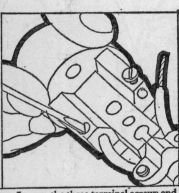

3 Loosen the three terminal screws and disconnect. Pull out flex leads.

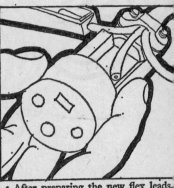

4 After preparing the new flex leads, place the cord through the collar into the grip and, using wire cutters, strip about ½ in. of covering from each lead.

5 Make sure that the earth lead is slightly longer than the neutral and live ones.

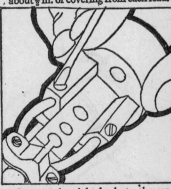

6 Connect the right leads to the respective terminals. Screw down tightly and then screw up the grip.

7 Slide the collar on to the connector and screw up tightly.

8 Finally plug into mains and test your new flex with the kettle.

re-wiring an older type of kettle connector

Most portable electrical appliances are fitted with flexible cords which are subject to hard wear. You should check all flexes periodically because breaks can soon become dangerous. A kettle connector should always be 3-core, 2.5 mm². Here's how to re-wire the older type of kettle connector.

WARNING: Make sure the flex is NOT connected to a plug IN A LIVE SOCKET when doing this repair.

1 A flexible cord often breaks here because of constant use.

2 Undo the earth clip screws on both sides with a screwdriver.

3 Remove the spring clips and carefully put them on one side. Swing aside the cord grip.

4 Remove fractured flex. Replace with new flex. First pull the earth lead (yellow/green) through the slot.

5 Make a neat loop with the wire. The earth clips fit on top.

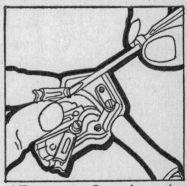

6 Turn case over. Connect brown wire to live terminal, blue wire to neutral terminal. Screw tightly.

7 Check wires are to correct terminals. Leave no loose wires. Join cases and re-screw earth clips.

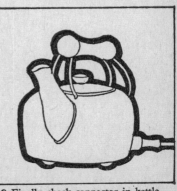

8 Finally check connector in kettle.

checking a faulty iron

Here are simple repairs you can do to a dry electric iron. Other repairs, such as repairing the element, should be done by a registered electrician. This is only one type of iron, but the principles apply to other makes:

WARNING: ALWAYS MAKE SURE THE PLUG IS DISCONNECTED FROM THE MAINS BEFORE CARRYING OUT ANY REPAIRS.

Remember the colour code for new flex — Green/Yellow — earth: Brown — live: Blue — neutral.

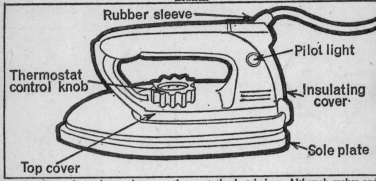

1 This shows the various points on a thermostatic electric iron. Although makes and designs differ, the essential points are the same. Not shown here is the element usually located in the sole plate.

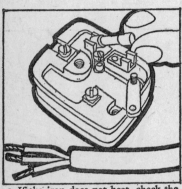

2 If the iron does not heat, check the mains plug to see if there are any loose wires, or if the plug is cracked.

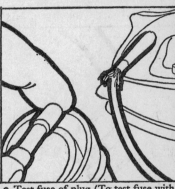

3 Test fuse of plug (To test fuse with torch battery and lamp *see* Mending a Fuse on page 76). Look for any broken wires in the cord near the rubber sleeve where much pulling and twisting takes place.

4 If the pilot light does not light, or flickers, switch off and disconnect plug. Unscrew the back insulating cover.

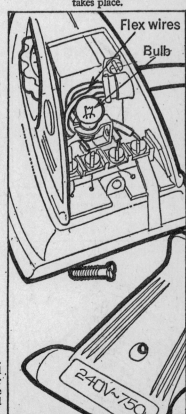

5 Unscrew bulb and test in a torch. Replace it if it is no good. Check cord connection to see if any are loose or worn. Should cord need replacing, note connections to respective terminals and fit new cord in the same manner.

Fixing
and
Joining

fixing to walls and ceilings

Here are some examples which. handymen will find useful when they need to hang weighty objects. Cavity walls and panels do not take screws easily, and offer no anchorage and, in the case of flush doors, the plywood is too thin to take a screw.

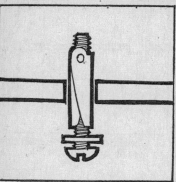

1 A spring toggle with two arms which spread the load over a wide area. Useful for lath and plaster ceilings or plasterboard and flush panel doors.

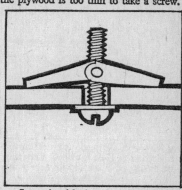

2 Insert it with the wings folded back. These will spring open on the other side of the board. Sizes from $\frac{1}{8}$ in. $\frac{1}{4}$ in. diameter, up to $2\frac{1}{2}$ in. long.

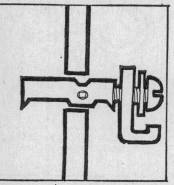

3 A gravity toggle suitable for fixing to wall boards or a narrow corner in a cavity wall.

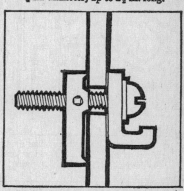

4 Push pivot arm through the hole and let it fall into a vertical position. Tighten it until toggle is hard up against reverse side. Sizes $\frac{1}{8}$ in. $-\frac{1}{4}$ in. diameter, 3 in. long.

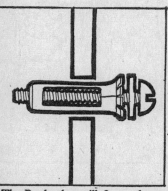

The Rawlanchor will fix to plaster board. The screw can be removed, and replaced which is an added advantage.

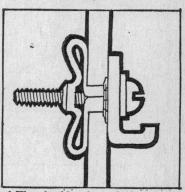

6 The shoulder draws back towards the bolt and grips the reverse side tightly. Sizes $\frac{1}{8}$ in. $-\frac{1}{4}$ in. diameter, up to $2\frac{1}{4}$ in. long.

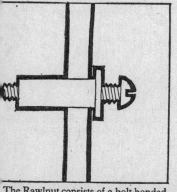

The Rawlnut consists of a bolt bonded to a rubber sleeve, suitable for combatting vibration. This type can easily be removed and used again.

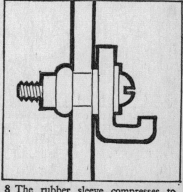

8 The rubber sleeve compresses to make a tight shoulder on the reverse side of the panel. Sizes $\frac{1}{8}$ in. $-\frac{1}{2}$ in diameter, and up to 2 ins. long.

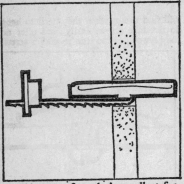

9 This type of toggle is excellent for cavity fixing. Hole is drilled. Retaining bar is slipped into hole with help of the nylon stop.

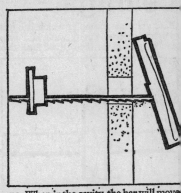

10 When in the cavity, the bar will move at right angles to the hole.

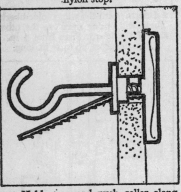

11 Hold strap and push collar along to fit into the hole. With sleeve and toggle bar tight, insert screw fixing.

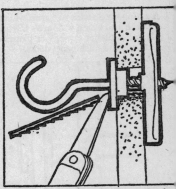

12 Cut off the exposed pieces of nylon strip close up to the sleeve.

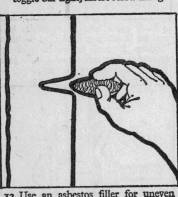

13 Use an asbestos filler for uneven holes. First moisten and roll into a plug.

14 Ram the filler firmly into the hole with tool supplied.

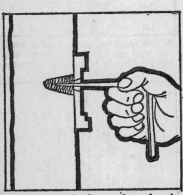

15 Drill hole in fixture then place in position. Insert the sharp end of tool for receiving the screw.

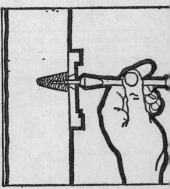

16 Place in screw through the fixture and drive home tightly.

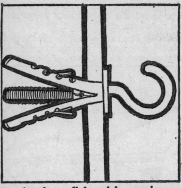

17 A nylon wallplug giving maximum expansion at inner end of fixing suitable for thin walls.

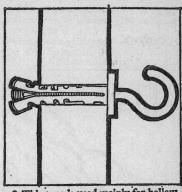

18 This type is used mainly for hollow block walls.

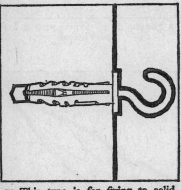

19 This type is for fixing to solid materials.

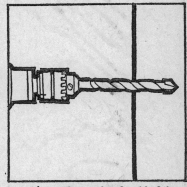

20 Stages of operation for this fixing. First drill the hole to the required size.

21 Insert the wallplug which has a hook-eye or nut, whichever you use.

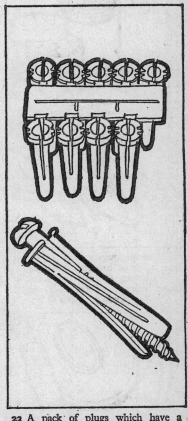

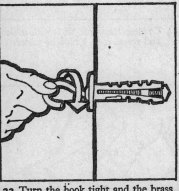

22 Turn the hook tight and the brass wedge will be drawn into the wallplug, expanding as it goes to give a strong grip.

23 A pack of plugs which have a smooth plastic outer surface to allow maximum contact area with a fin to prevent rotation when the screw is inserted.

joining metal by soldering

Soldering will give you a strong, safe joint when you want to join two pieces of metal together. It is essential to clean the work to be joined and to work with the correct size of iron and the right heat.

WARNING: When using a corrosive flux, thoroughly clean afterwards by rinsing in a hot soda solution (1 tablespoon soda to ½ pt. water), then dry off. If using a blowlamp, keep away from inflammable liquids. *Acid fluxes must not be used on electrical connections.*

1 Soldering equipment: *1.* Types of iron. *2.* Rapid heating soldering iron. *3.* Liquid flux. *4.* Cored solder. *5.* Flux strips, tinsman solder, emery cloth. *6.* Wire brush. *7.* Types of bit.

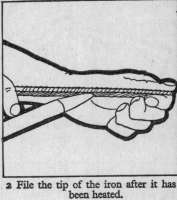

2 File the tip of the iron after it has been heated.

3 How the tip slope of an iron should look, not a sharp point but more a chisel shape.

4 To clean the point, tin it with solder and rotate it in a blob of solder.

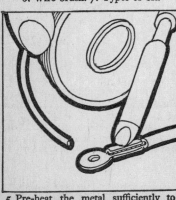

5 Pre-heat the metal sufficiently to melt solder (if not hot enough you'll get a cold joint). Use a rosin-core solder on electrical work.

6 An acid flux cleans the surface and keeps heat from oxidizing surface before solder is applied. Wash off excess afterwards.

7 Tin surfaces with solder after cleaning to a shiny brightness. Join together and re-heat.

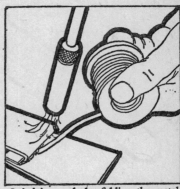

8 A joint made by folding the metal at the ends. Interlock by hammering flat and flowing the solder down one edge.

9 Always clean the joints with wire brush. Use emery cloth which will remove all dirt and grease from the surface, otherwise a weak joint will result.

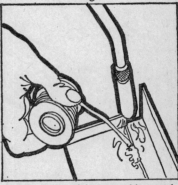

10 For a large joint use a blow-torch for more heat. Tin both surfaces then re-heat with iron, flowing the solder along the seam.

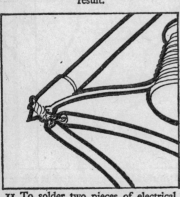

11 To solder two pieces of electrical wire, tin the wires, twist together and apply solder.

12 Another type of joint with two electrical wires interwoven. These can be soldered.

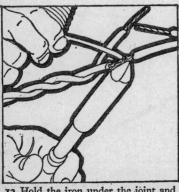

13 Hold the iron under the joint and feed the solder on to joint. Let it melt and flow until joint is covered. Allow to cool before wiring.

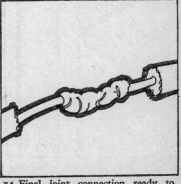

14 Final joint connection ready to take the flex sheaf. This joint is as strong as if the wire had not been cut.

woodworking joints

Here are some of the basic joints in wood. Some are more difficult to make than others but there is no reason why you should not be able to tackle any of them given the right tools.

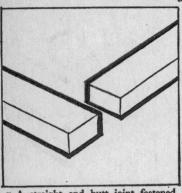

1 A straight end butt joint fastened together with glue, screws or nails.

•2 A mitre joint used for frames. The angle of 45° is cut in a mitre box.

3 Halving joint. Two pieces cross each other and the surfaces are flush.

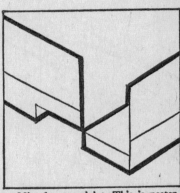

4 Mitred corner joint. This is neater than the simple cross lap joint.

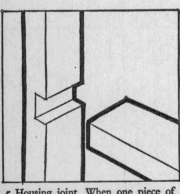

5 Housing joint. When one piece of wood is let into the body of another it is said to be housed.

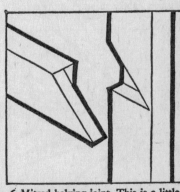

6 Mitred halving joint. This is a little more difficult to make.

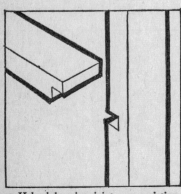

7 Halved housing joint – a variation of 5.

8 Angled halving joint.

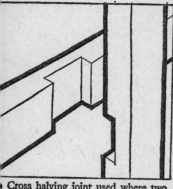

Cross halving joint used where two members in a framework cross each other.

10 Dovetail halved joint. This joint resists outward strain owing to wedge shaped side.

Tee halving joint. A simple way to make a right angled joint.

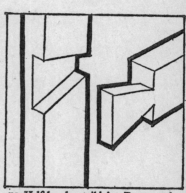

12 Half-lap dovetail joint. Best to make a template from a thin piece of sheet-metal to make this joint.

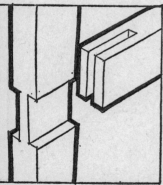

Tee bridle joint. Useful joint in furniture as a cross rail.

14 Dovetail housing joint. Both sides of the dovetail are cut to the angles from a template.

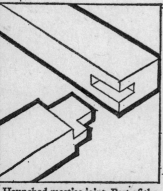

Haunched mortise joint. Part of the mortise breaks through the end of the timber preventing twisting.

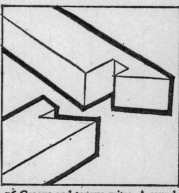

16 Groove and tongue mitre. A sound joint but requires some skill to make. No room for adjustment once cut.

Carpets and Flooring

lifting floorboards

At some time the floorboards in your house will have to be lifted either to inspect the electric cables or gas pipes or to repair damaged floorboards. Badly nailed floorboards are unsightly. Here's how to make a good job.

WARNING: TURN OFF GAS, ELECTRICITY AND WATER BEFORE COMMENCING ANY CUTTING BECAUSE OF ANY ELECTRIC CABLES OR PIPES THAT MAY BE BELOW.

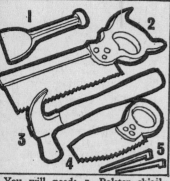

You will need: 1. Bolster chisel. 2. Tenon saw. 3. Hammer. 4. Flooring saw. 5. Flooring brads.

2 Insert a bolster chisel just near the end of a floorboard and tap gently down.

Use a levering action in combination with the hammer and apply outward pressure.

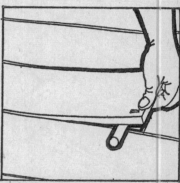

4 As the nails are levered out, slide a rod underneath the board.

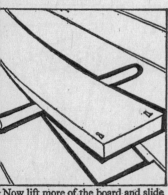

Now lift more of the board and slide the rod further along.

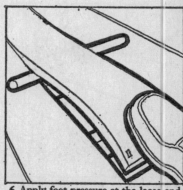

6 Apply foot pressure at the loose end of the board and the nails will start to give further along past the rod.

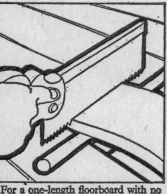

For a one-length floorboard with no joint, lever it up and find a joist where nails appear. Position rod near and cut cleanly across with tenon saw.

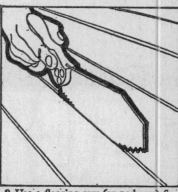

8 Use a flooring saw (or pad saw) for tongued and grooved floorboards. Gently cut along one side of the board, keeping saw horizontal, then lift.

curing squeaky floorboards

Boards which rub together when trodden on cause squeaks. Perhaps the electrician or plumber took the boards up and replaced them with the nails in the original holes. Here is how to take the squeak out of your floor or staircase.

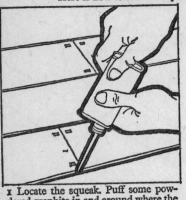

1 Locate the squeak. Puff some powdered graphite in and around where the nails are.

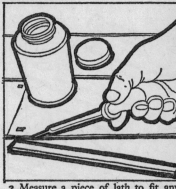

2 Measure a piece of lath to fit any gap and inject glue along crevice. Thinly glue lath.

3 Tap the lath home into the gap and allow to set. This will take up any side movement of the floorboards.

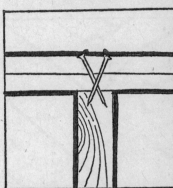

4 Remove any loose nails at joists and drive home new nails at angles in new positions as shown.

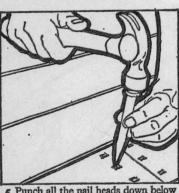

5 Punch all the nail heads down below the surface and fill old holes with wood filler.

6 If accessible, hammer home a wedge below floor, between joist and floor board.

7 Add a supporting member between two joists to support a creaking floorboard.

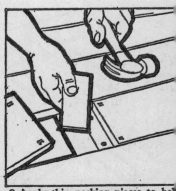

8 Apply thin packing pieces to help keep floorboards level.

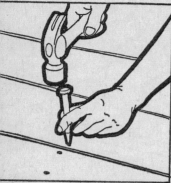

If the nails do not stop the squeak,
y screws. Start by indenting the wood
$\frac{1}{2}$ in. away from the nail hole.

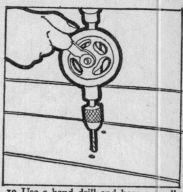

10 Use a hand drill and bore a small
hole at each indentation to take the
screws and countersink.

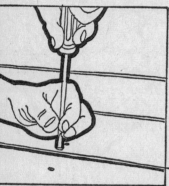

Drive home each screw tightly until
countersunk.

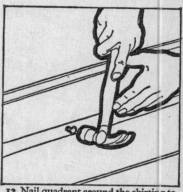

12 Nail quadrant around the skirting to
stop movement of boards in this particular area.

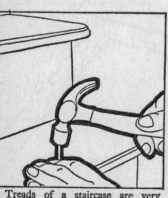

Treads of a staircase are very
bject to noise and squeak. Nail or
ew if you cannot get access under the
stairs.

14 If possible to get under the stairs,
hammer home wedges precoated with
glue between treads and stringers. Then
nail.

Hammer in any loose blocks under
treads. Even put in new ones glued
d nailed. Fix anything that moves.

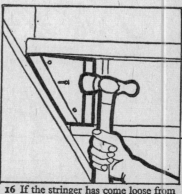

16 If the stringer has come loose from
the wall, nail it back or use rawlplugs
and screws.

laying parquet flooring

A good foundation is of the utmost importance in this operation. If concrete, then al'
hollows and bumps must be attended to. If floor boards, remove all high spots by plane
Punch nails below the surface. Surface a very old floor with sheet hardboard, rough sid.
uppermost. Lay blocks starting from the centre and string chalk lines. If you star
at the edge check edges are straight. Keep hardwoods or selected pine blocks indoor
for several days before laying, to adjust moisture content.

1 You will need: *1*. Electric drill. *2*. Hammer. *3*. Sharp knife. *4*. Brush. *5*. Sanding disc
6. Knocking up block. *7*. Knocking up tool.

2 After preparing the floor apply recommended adhesive thinly where you
are laying blocks. Slide each block into
planned pattern.

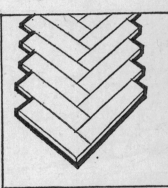

3 Some parquet blocks have a thi
veneer of hardwood and a soft ba
others have a built-in adhesive. Abov
is shown a herringbone pattern.

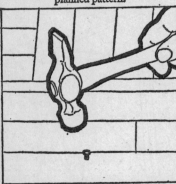

4 Where the new floor meets a doorway
use a bevelled moulding strip. Stick
with adhesive and panel pin at intervals.

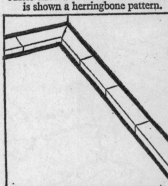

5 Lay a line of blocks between ea
wall to allow for slight expansion. T
reduces number of blocks to be c

6 When the parquet floor has been
laid, sand it to get rid of any uneven-
ness in the blocks.

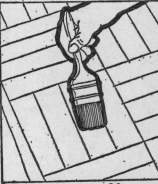

7 Apply three coats of lacquer g
with a soft brush. Then the floor
only need a wipe over occasion

Interlocking Parquet panels can be laid over any type of sub-floor. No sticking or fastening down is required. Each panel interlocks with tongued and grooved joints.

Lay the cork underlay over the moisture barrier film on a concrete sub-floor. Note expansion gap left.

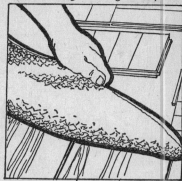

9 Treat wooden floors for protruding nails. Lay cork underlay in suitable lengths, cork side down. Leave ½ in. expansion gap round each.

Assemble a number of panels in position using a knocking-up block. Place in one corner and add. See that each joint is close fitting.

11 This shows the special knocking-up tool in a position near the skirting board that does not allow free use of the hammer.

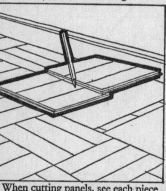

When cutting panels, see each piece has a tongue or groove to fit the full panel and maintain the basket pattern. Use hand saw.

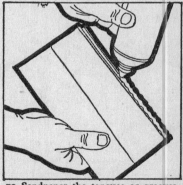

13 Sandpaper the tongues or grooves of the cut pieces. Spread on adhesive and slide into position. Cut tongues off alternate panels when butting to skirting.

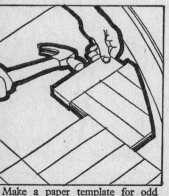

Make a paper template for odd shapes to use as a guide when cutting the panel.

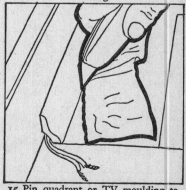

15 Pin quadrant or TV·moulding to the skirting with panel pins. Trim surplus moisture barrier film when moulding is fixed.

laying a hardboard floor

Laying expensive carpets, tiles or linoleum over badly worn floorboards will do n[o] good to them. Every mark will wear through under pressure. Hardboard sheets ove[r] the floor will provide a good underlay for the floor covering. Buy sheets of hardboar[d] 8 ft. by 4 ft., cut these in half and you will have manageable 4 ft. squares. *REMEMBE[R] to lay the hardboard sheets rough side up if laying tiles on top.*

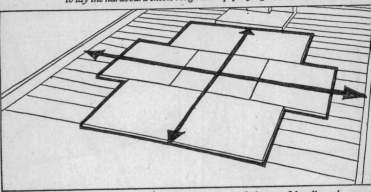

1 First measure the room to estimate the number of sheets of hardboard you w[ill] need. Find the centre points of the room by stringing a chalk line. Lay a few she[ets] experimentally. Note how the joints are staggered.

2 Prepare the old floor boards. Take up any old tacks or nails. Hammer home small raised ones. Generally clean the surface.

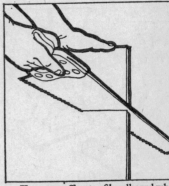

3 Keep any off-cuts of hardboard wh[ich] will come in useful at the edges of [the] room.

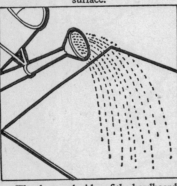

4 Wet the rough sides of the hardboard and then leave for about 24 hours to condition.

5 Lay first square in centre of room [as] shown in illustration 1. Nail at 4[in.] intervals all over the board starting fr[om] the near edge.

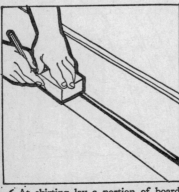

6 At skirting lay a portion of board over the last nailed board and against the skirting. With a block of wood, pencil a line coinciding with the skirting.

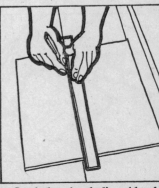

7 Cut the board to the line with a sha[rp] knife. Push it against the skirting a[nd] cut the board flush with the nail[ed] square. Continue all round the roo[m.]

re-surfacing an uneven floor

ou can re-surface all kinds of sub-floors by the use of a rapid hardening powder ixed with water. It provides an easy-to-lay rapid hardening screed that finds its own vel to the thickness you require. It can be laid on concrete, wood, brick, flag, etc. The floor we describe below is concrete.

You will need. _1_. Powder mix. _2_. room. _3_. Old distemper brush. _4_. ucket and mixing stick. _5_. Steel trowel.

2 First clean any polish, grease or sharp projections from the floor. Use a small scraper.

Sweep clean any dirt or loose material which might impair adhesion.

4 Damp absorbent surfaces with water before applying the mix. Non-porous surfaces need a neoprene primer as recommended.

To _1_ volume of clean water in a ucket add 3 volumes of powder. Stir oroughly to a thick consistency. eave to stand 2 minutes. Use in 30 minutes.

6 Re-stir. Pour mix on to floor. Hold your steel trowel at an angle, grind it into the sub-floor and spread quickly to the thickness. Leave to find its own level.

8 The manufacturers of Ardit Z8 recommend the following coverage and treatment: The amount of Ardit Z8 needed depends on the thickness of application, but generally, 1 sq. yd. covered to a thickness of 1/16 in. requires $3\frac{1}{2}$ lbs. There are three Ardit Z8 bag sizes.

NOTE:

1 Mixed Ardit Z8 must be used within approx. 30 mins.

2 Where rising damp is suspected ask manufacturer for further information.

3 In warm conditions, damp down with water or cover with wet newspaper for a few hours once the Ardit Z8 is hard enough to walk on.

4 For a thickness over 3/16 in. mix with $2\frac{1}{2}$ volumes Ardex 1/12 in. or 1/8 in. aggregate or similar clean aggregate.

5 Seek manufacturer's advice before laying on old adhesives or damp-proof membranes.

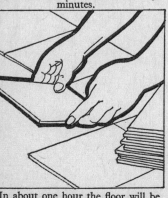

In about one hour the floor will be dy to walk on. You can lay tiles in ut 6 to 8 hours on a perfect level flooring.

laying linoleum sheet and tiles

Linoleum, if laid correctly, will give years of wear. It is no longer a dull and dreary floor covering. Most modern designs are very attractive. On poor floors it is best to have an underlay of felt paper or hardboard.

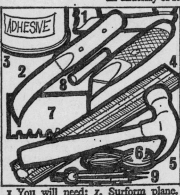

1 You will need: *1.* Surform plane. *2.* Lino knife. *3.* Adhesive. *4.* Folding rule. *5.* Hammer. *6.* String. *7.* Spreader. *8.* Chalk *9.* Compasses.

2 Measure with a rule and mark with pencil the shape of difficult mouldings on to the lino.

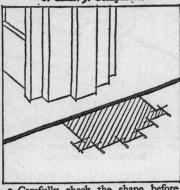

3 Carefully check the shape before cutting.

4 Cut out the shape with a lino knife. Keep slightly on the generous side.

5 Place the shape up to the moulding. It may need a bit more cutting.

6 Roll back lino. Spread adhesive over floor with a notched floor trowel. Keep the adhesive even and thin. When tacky roll lino back firmly.

7 A flexible moulding gauge made up of multi steel needles which take up any shape. Can be purchased in hardware shops.

8 This is a scriber which moves along mouldings to reproduce an exact outline by a sharp point.

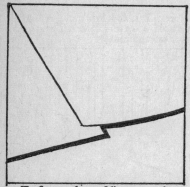

9 To fit one sheet of lino to another, overlap one piece by ½ in.

10 Cut through both thicknesses to get a perfect butt joint. Cut with a knife against a straight edge.

11 Old floorboards usually need some treatment. Remove old nails which have been badly hammered in.

12 Use a cleft tool to remove the most stubborn nails and tacks.

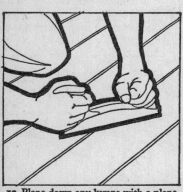

13 Plane down any lumps with a plane scraper. Remove old paint or grease.

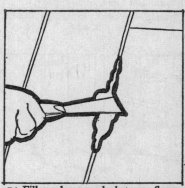

14 Fill any large cracks between floorboards with a suitable plastic or wood filler.

15 After all repairs clean the floor of any dust. Wash and apply a coat of floor size to seal the pores of the wood.

16 To lay lino tiles, measure opposite walls and mark a centre point. Chalk the string.

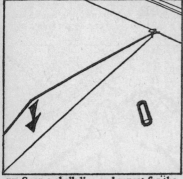

17 Snap a chalk line and repeat for the centre point of the other two walls.

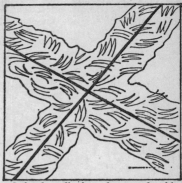

18 Apply adhesive along each side of your string marks.

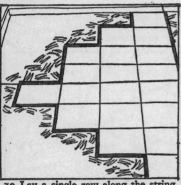

19 Lay a single row along the string line. Continue in a pyramid until all tiles are down in one half. Repeat for other half. Leave border until last.

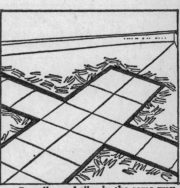

20 Lay diagonal tiles in the same way but start the chalk strings at the corners of the room.

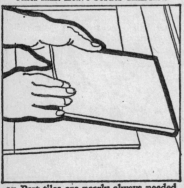

21 Part tiles are nearly always needed for skirting boards. To cut correct size lay the wall tile on top of a loose one.

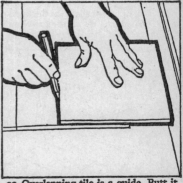

22 Overlapping tile is a guide. Butt it against skirting. Mark lower tile with pencil and cut. Stick down the complete tile, then the cut one.

23 To fit round radiator pipes. Measure centre of pipe from wall. With compass mark circle at this centre.

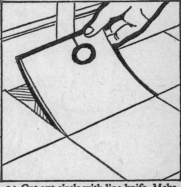

24 Cut out circle with lino knife. Make a slit from hole to the edge of the tile and fit into place.

laying carpets

Always buy a carpet which has a brand name. This will almost certainly guarantee that you get a good one. Some carpets need an underlay which helps to promote a longer life, while others have their own built in underlay of latex.

WARNING: The use of a "knee kicker" requires some skill in use. Uneven kicking can cause buckling and damage to the carpet. It is inadvisable to fit a carpet with a built in underlay to gripper strips.

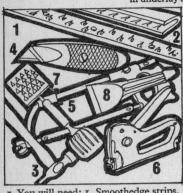

1 You will need: *1*. Smoothedge strips. *2*. Metal edging strips. *3*. Hammer. *4*. Sharp knife. *5*. Hacksaw. *6*. Staple gun. *7*. Knee kicker. *8*. Bolster chisel.

2 Lay the edging strip, a thin lath of wood with gripping spikes, with the spikes towards the skirting. Nail them round the room in 4 ft. lengths.

3 Position the strips about the thickness of the carpet from the skirting to allow raw edges to be tucked down.

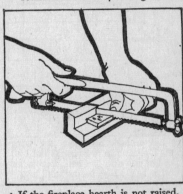

4 If the fireplace hearth is not raised, metal strips can be used. Mitre the corners of these for a good fit.

5 Lay the cut pieces of metal strip round the hearth and across the door width. Nail through the slots provided.

6 Start placing the underlay – this is a rubber type. Lay cushion side down working from the door threshold.

7 The first edge should run even with the strip. Adjust from the door wall edge to allow for any cutting.

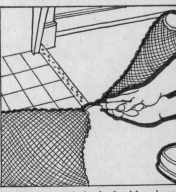

8 Trim the underlay back with a sharp knife at the hearth, clear of the grippers.

9 Distribute the underlay in all directions by pushing evenly with your hands.

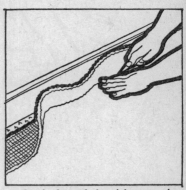

10 Staple the underlay right up to the edge of the gripper strips. Now cut off any surplus.

11 With a sharp knife trim off the surplus at the hearth and remove.

12 Follow round the entire room cutting cleanly to the strips and finish stapling to the floor.

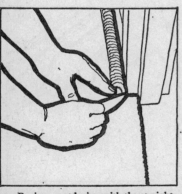

13 Begin carpet laying with the straight carpet to wall. Run inside the door to the rebate and trim back.

14 Use the knee kicker to force the carpet in the direction of the doorway and towards the edging strip.

15 Trim off at the threshold of the door and work edges over the spikes and into the channel.

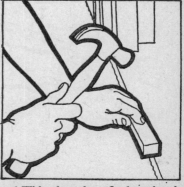

16 With the edges firmly gripped hammer down the lip of the metal gripper. Use a block of wood to take the hammer.

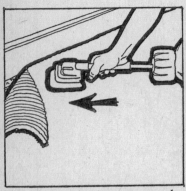

17 Now stretch the carpet at the opposite side of the room (see final illustration) for a small distance.

18 Repeat at opposite side, again working a small distance. Continue until carpet is stretched at all walls.

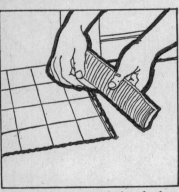

19 Trim the carpet at the hearth edges after kicking on to the gripper strips.

20 Now apply the same procedure as at the threshold of the door, going all round the hearth.

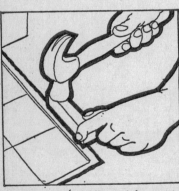

21 Close the metal lip over the carpet, using the block of wood to take the hammer.

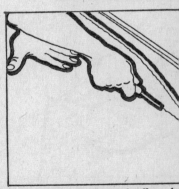

22 Using a bradawl, mark off surplus carpet into space between gripper strips and skirting. Cut to fit. Special carpet trimmers can do this job.

23 Force the trimmed edge down in the gap between gripper strips and skirting with a bolster chisel.

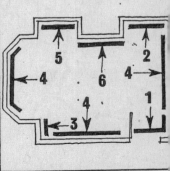

24 Here is a plan of the room showing the order in which the stretching should be done.

laying a stair carpet

You need a good quality carpet to stand up to stairway traffic. Laying a carpet correctly over a good underlay will ensure hard wear, soft tread, and less noise. Always lay a stair carpet with the pile in the correct direction so that brushing up the stairs will raise the pile; brushing down will flatten it.

Measure from the top riser, across the tread, over the nosing to the next riser to the bottom for approximate measurement. Add 20 in. to allow movement of carpet up and down to even out wear.

2 Always fasten the stair underlay to overhang the nosing which gets the most wear. Allow for stair rods or clips of about 1 in. gap.

Using carpet grippers, place these on top of the underlay and nail or screw into the tread.

4 Tack carpet at top of stairs over the underlay. Move down one tread at a time, pressing carpet firmly into angle of gripper.

Press the special stretching tool supplied with the gripper strip with the squared end into the angle for full engagement.

6 On bends the carpet's horizontal threads must run parallel to the nosing. Fold up surplus on the narrow side into a narrow pleat and tack under the nosing.

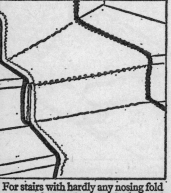

For stairs with hardly any nosing fold the carpet into a downward pleat and tack into the angle between tread and riser.

8 At the bottom riser, form a pleat and tack well along the bottom angle as shown.

repairs to a carpet

Carpets take a lot of punishment and parts of them can soon wear or be stained, or even worse burnt by a carelessly dropped cigarette or a spark from the fire. The remedy for this unsightly appearance is to insert a new patch. If you haven't any spare matching portions you will have to buy a remnant from the shop where you bought the carpet. Here we deal with a non-fitted carpet.

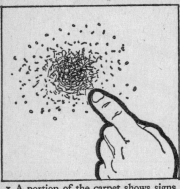

1 A portion of the carpet shows signs of wear or perhaps has a hole in it.

2 Turn the carpet over to the back and mark a square over the damaged area.

3 Place a board under the hole and with a sharp knife cut a clean square out.

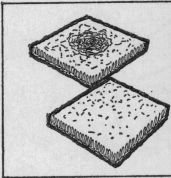

4 Now match up a similar square of carpet and cut cleanly to the same size.

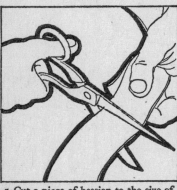

5 Cut a piece of hessian to the size of the hole, or two if necessary, approximately 1 in. larger round than the hole.

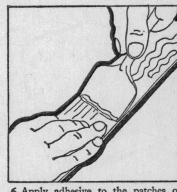

6 Apply adhesive to the patches of hessian.

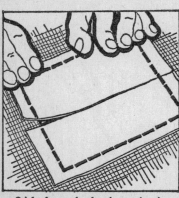

7 Stick down the hessian strips into place over the hole as shown.

8 Apply adhesive along edges of patch and underneath. Turn carpet over and press patch into place. Try to get the pile in the same direction.

care of your carpets

)nce a carpet has been laid it will shed fluff. After the first vacuum clean, do not lean again for a week or two, to allow the carpet to settle and the loose tufts and ends o fall down into the base of the pile. You can now vacuum clean regularly to remove irt and dust. You will need to clean your carpet occasionally. There are several hampoos on the market that will do the job, but it will pay you to have your carpet rofessionally cleaned once in a while.

A QUICK-TO-ESTIMATE ROOM RECKONER IN SQ. YDS.

f your room is, say, 7 ft. 6 in. wide by 9 ft. long, look down the 7 ft. 6 in. width olumn to 9 ft. length. The figure is $7\frac{1}{2}$ sq. yds.

LENGTH		WIDTH				
ft.	in.	6 ft. sq. yd.	7 ft. 6 in. sq. yd.	9 ft. sq. yd.	10 ft. 6 in. sq. yd.	12 ft. sq. yd.
6	0	4	5	6	7	8
6	6	$4\frac{1}{3}$	$5\frac{5}{12}$	$6\frac{1}{2}$	$7\frac{7}{12}$	$8\frac{2}{3}$
7	0	$4\frac{2}{3}$	$5\frac{5}{6}$	7	$8\frac{1}{6}$	$9\frac{1}{3}$
7	6	5	$6\frac{1}{4}$	$7\frac{1}{2}$	$8\frac{3}{4}$	10
8	0	$5\frac{1}{3}$	$6\frac{2}{3}$	8	$9\frac{1}{3}$	$10\frac{2}{3}$
8	6	$5\frac{2}{3}$	$7\frac{1}{12}$	$8\frac{1}{2}$	$9\frac{11}{12}$	$11\frac{1}{3}$
9	0	6	$7\frac{1}{2}$	9	$10\frac{1}{2}$	12
9	6	$6\frac{1}{3}$	$7\frac{11}{12}$	$9\frac{1}{2}$	$11\frac{1}{12}$	$12\frac{2}{3}$
10	0	$6\frac{2}{3}$	$8\frac{1}{3}$	10	$11\frac{2}{3}$	$13\frac{1}{3}$
10	6	7	$8\frac{3}{4}$	$10\frac{1}{2}$	$12\frac{1}{4}$	14
11	0	$7\frac{1}{3}$	$9\frac{1}{6}$	11	$12\frac{5}{6}$	$14\frac{2}{3}$
11	6	$7\frac{2}{3}$	$9\frac{7}{12}$	$11\frac{1}{2}$	$13\frac{5}{12}$	$15\frac{1}{3}$
12	0	8	10	12	14	16
12	6	$8\frac{1}{3}$	$10\frac{5}{12}$	$12\frac{1}{2}$	$14\frac{7}{12}$	$16\frac{2}{3}$
13	0	$8\frac{2}{3}$	$10\frac{5}{6}$	13	$15\frac{1}{6}$	$17\frac{1}{3}$
13	6	9	$11\frac{1}{4}$	$13\frac{1}{2}$	$15\frac{3}{4}$	18
14	0	$9\frac{1}{3}$	$11\frac{2}{3}$	14	$16\frac{1}{3}$	$18\frac{2}{3}$
14	6	$9\frac{2}{3}$	$12\frac{1}{12}$	$14\frac{1}{2}$	$16\frac{11}{12}$	$19\frac{1}{3}$
15	0	10	$12\frac{1}{2}$	15	$17\frac{1}{2}$	20
15	6	$10\frac{1}{3}$	$12\frac{11}{12}$	$15\frac{1}{2}$	$18\frac{1}{12}$	$20\frac{2}{3}$
16	0	$10\frac{2}{3}$	$13\frac{1}{3}$	16	$18\frac{2}{3}$	$21\frac{1}{3}$

Furniture and Woodwork

framing your pictures

Pictures, far more than anything else, lend originality to a room. You can get a great deal of satisfaction out of making your own picture frames with the right tools and using the many beautiful mouldings that are available.

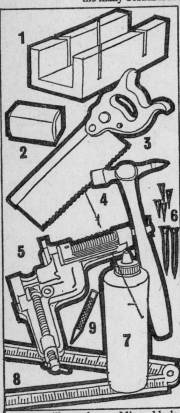

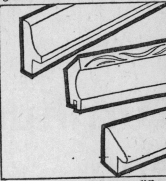

2 These are three of the many different frame mouldings available for you to choose from.

1 You will need: *1.* Mitre block. *2.* Sandpaper block. *3.* Tenon saw. *4.* Light hammer. *5.* Mitre cramp. *6.* Panel pins and brads. *7.* Adhesive. *8.* Folding rule. *9.* Nail punch.

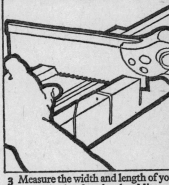

3 Measure the width and length of your picture allowing for a border. Mitre one end of the moulding.

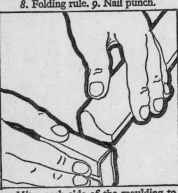

4 Mitre each side of the moulding to your measurements and smooth the ends with a fine sandpaper.

5 Apply adhesive thinly to each mitre joint.

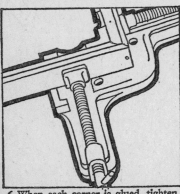

6 When each corner is glued, tighten each side in the mitre cramp. Make a hole with a bradawl. Panel pin each corner, but don't drive right home.

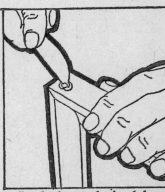

7 Punch the panel pins below the surface with a nail punch. Fill the holes with a plastic wood or cellulose filler.

8 When the filler has set, sandpaper smooth the whole of the frame.

9 Measure length and width of inside back frame. Cut to size a backing for the frame from hardboard or stout card.

10 Turn the frame over. Put your picture in first then the backing. Hammer the brads into position, leaving them projecting slightly.

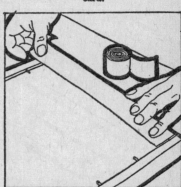

11 Cover the brads with a strip of masking tape or brown gummed paper.

hanging your pictures

When framing pictures bear in mind the position in which they are to be hung. In a modern room the frames should suit the furnishing scheme. Flat frames which harmonize with the colour scheme are best. Ornate frames do not normally mix well with modern decor.

Historical subjects and landscapes are best hung in a hall or on a staircase. Oil paintings require well recessed frames with more ornate carvings. Allow a narrow frame for a black and white subject, a slightly larger one for water colour, and a heavier type for an oil painting.

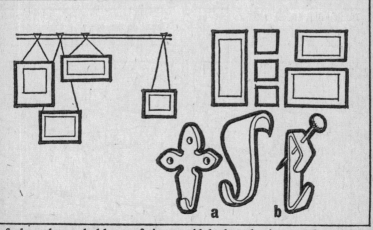

Left above shows a bad layout of pictures with hooks and strings prominent. Right above shows a much better balanced and orderly arrangement. *a*. 2 types of brass hooks for picture rails. *b*. a picture hook with a very strong steel pin which makes only a tiny hole in the wall.

117

putting up shelves

If you haven't enough shelf space you can easily make more yourself. They can be fitted in alcoves, cupboards, pantry, garage or shed. Here are a few examples.

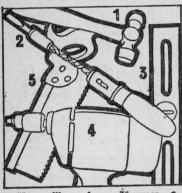

1 You will need: 1. Hammer. 2. Screwdriver. 3. Spirit level. 4. Electric or hand drill 5. Tenon saw.

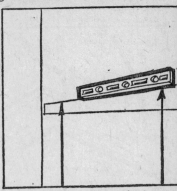

2 Shelves must be level. Place a support baton against the wall to the required height, adjust with spirit level and mark a horizontal line with a pencil.

3 For alcove shelves measure the length and width. Allow for the side support members' thickness. Cut timbers to length, drill holes about 1½ in. at each end at even intervals. Countersink each hole.

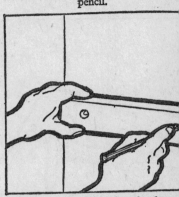

4 Place back support against the alcove wall and with a pencil mark accurately the centres of the drilled holes.

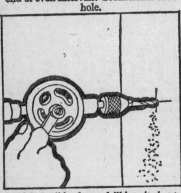

5 If the wall is plaster drill into it about 1 in. to take the wood wallplugs. If brick use a masonry drill.

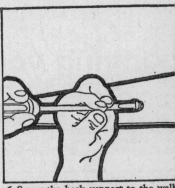

6 Screw the back support to the wall. Check once more with the spirit level that it is true.

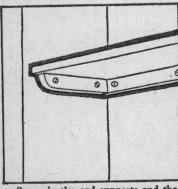

7 Screw in the end supports and the shelf can now seat itself on top. For more security screw it into the back and side supports.

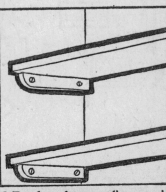

8 For short alcoves or distances, side supports only are needed.

9 This is a more advanced type of shelving – an 'egg-crate' open system of construction which looks very attractive in an alcove. Measure up the length and width of the alcove and cut the end supports, as before. Use a spirit level and fix to alcove sides.

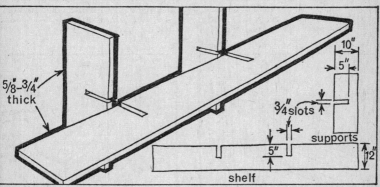

10 The frame can be made up with $\frac{5}{8}$ in. or $\frac{3}{4}$ in. plywood or veneered hardboards. Cut the two uprights and joints to fit vertically inside the unit. Then cut the centre shelf with slots exactly coinciding with the uprights. Make sure to cut the slots accurately. Cut the top and bottom shelves. Fix these to the side supports with $1\frac{3}{4}$ in. flat head wood screws, countersunk and filled with wood filler.

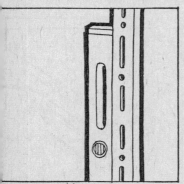

11 Readymade shelves have frames of slotted aluminium and supports. Always get a true vertical between frames when fixing and check horizontal.

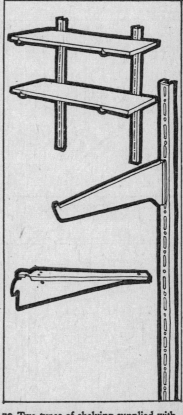

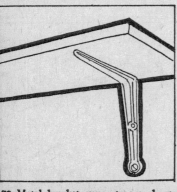

12 Metal bracket supports are cheap to buy. This type of shelf can be put up very quickly. Very suitable for garage or shed.

13 Two types of shelving supplied with supports. Very elegant, slim and strong.

timber repairs with metal plates

Splits, fractures or loose joints in wood can be difficult or impossible to repair with glue. Steel or brass repair plates, in various shapes, can make a quick, easy and permanent joint. They can be painted to match the woodwork or recessed and covered over with wood filler.

1 A straight mending plate forms a strong joint. You will need joints, screws, screwdriver, wood filler.

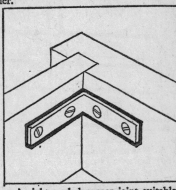

2 A right-angled corner joint suitable for a drawer.

3 An angled plate used on a defective window joint.

4 A right-angled plate for a frame.

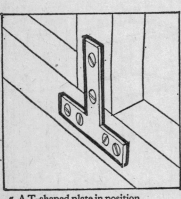

5 A T-shaped plate in position.

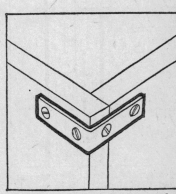

6 A right-angled plate to strengthen the corners of a box.

7 A strong plate used to hold a loose joint in a garden gate.

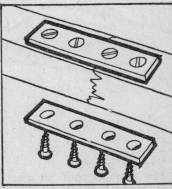

8 Use a plate on both sides, secure with screws for a fracture right through the wood.

9 A heavier type of metal plate used to support a garden gate post. The plates are sunk to a depth of about 8 in. and screwed to the post.

10 An angled metal plate used to repair a broken arris rail.

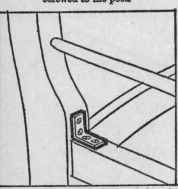

11 The base of a chair can be reinforced with a small angled plate. Because this is out of sight it needs no recessing.

12 Fitted plates for fractures at the bottom of chair seats must be recessed, but do not need filling.

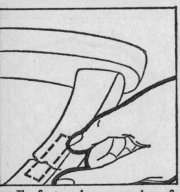

13 For fractures in cross-members of chairs, pencil a shape from the outline of the plate.

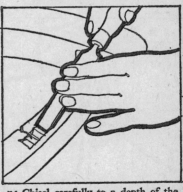

14 Chisel carefully to a depth of the thickness of the plate plus 1/16th in. more.

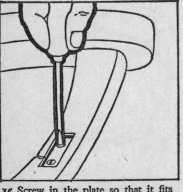

15 Screw in the plate so that it fits square and tight.

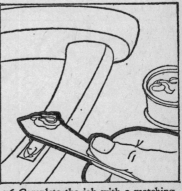

16 Complete the job with a matching wood filler.

re-upholstering
a worn seat

An old, tatty seat can be given a new lease of life by re-upholstering it with a new material. Follow the steps below and you'll wonder why you haven't tried this before.

1 You will need 1. Hammer. 2. Large scissors. 3. Pencil. 4. Ruler. 5. 1 in. thick slabs of foam rubber. 6. Cotton cloth. 7. Bag of polythene chips. 8. Brading and material. Piece of muslin (not shown).

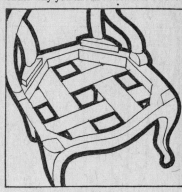

2 Remove the old seating down to the cross webbing. Check the web for strength and if not strong enough, renew it (see webbing page 124).

3 Place a sheet of paper over the webbing, hold firmly and trace an outline of the inside of the chair.

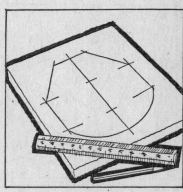

4 Transfer the outline on to two slabs of foam rubber.

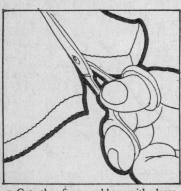

5 Cut the foam rubber with large scissors to the traced outline.

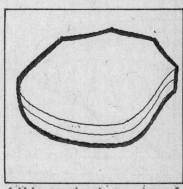

6 Make sure that the two pieces of foam rubber are identical.

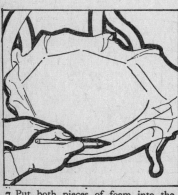

7 Put both pieces of foam into the seat. Now place another piece of paper over the top and trace the outline of the seat top.

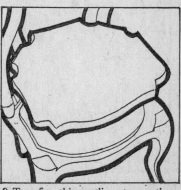

8 Transfer this outline to another piece of foam. Cut out as before. Place this over the other two pieces of foam rubber.

9 Sprinkle small pieces of foam rubber chips over the seat. Buy your polythene chips from any DIY shop.

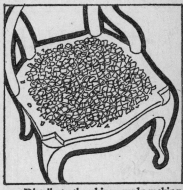

10 Distribute the chips evenly making a higher mound in the centre of the seat.

11 Cover with a light cotton sheet to keep the chips in place.

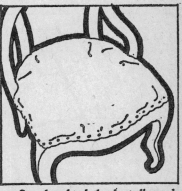

12 Stretch and tack the sheet all round with small furniture tacks. Trim off surplus.

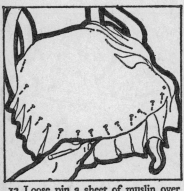

13 Loose pin a sheet of muslin over the cotton sheet and mark with a pencil along the bottom edge.

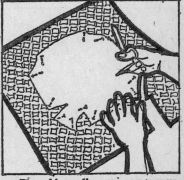

14 Place this muslin pattern on to your material. Cut round it with scissors allowing about ½ in. beyond the edge of the pattern.

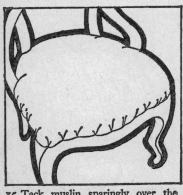

15 Tack muslin sparingly over the cotton sheet just enough to hold.

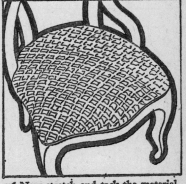

16 Now stretch and tack the material firmly all round the seat. Trim finally with braid, using gimbel tacks to secure.

renewing the webbing of a chair

The webbing beneath seats of chairs sometimes breaks or becomes so stretched that the chair is most uncomfortable to sit on or indeed dangerous. By renewing the webbing in rubber latex as shown here the chair can be made comfortable once more.

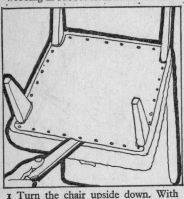

1 Turn the chair upside down. With an old chisel remove all the tacks and hessian cover.

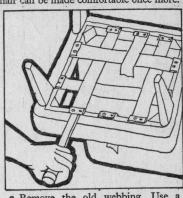

2 Remove the old webbing. Use a mallet and chisel to prize up the holding tacks.

3 Take the new webbing and tack one end to the side of the chair as shown. Now stretch the webbing.

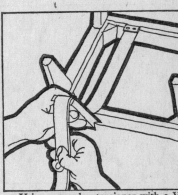

4 Using a wooden tensioner with a V notch at one end (you can make this yourself) pull the webbing taut.

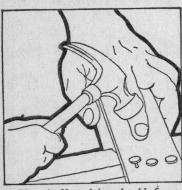

5 Place the V notch into the side frame and tension. Drive say, three tacks down.

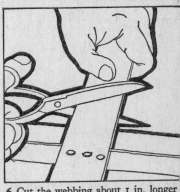

6 Cut the webbing about 1 in. longer than the frame and tuck over, placing a couple of tacks to secure.

7 Continue in the same way with the rest of the webbing, putting the strips in the same position as the old ones.

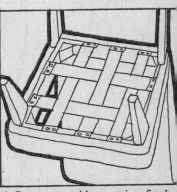

8 Cross-weave with two strips of webbing; tension up as before. Finally cover with new hessian.

small repairs to furnishing fabrics

Furnishing fabrics take a good deal of wear and tear and accidents will happen. Sometimes it is necessary to repair a hole or cut which looks untidy and threadbare. Here we show how to repair a small cut in a leather chair. You can also treat tapestry or other material in the same way.

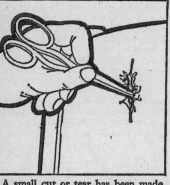

1 A small cut or tear has been made in your leather upholstery. Start by tucking back any loose filling.

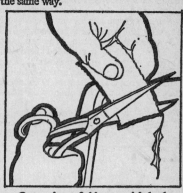

2 Cut a piece of thin material, leather if possible, just longer and wider than the cut.

3 Very carefully insert the patch of leather into the cut opening. Press against the filling so that it lies flat, covering the tear.

4 Pull back the torn edges and apply an adhesive used for sticking leather. You can obtain this from most DIY shops.

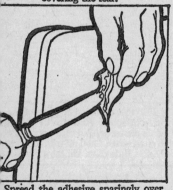

5 Spread the adhesive sparingly over the patch and sides of tear and allow to get tacky.

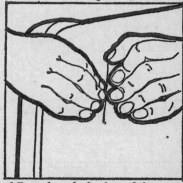

6 Press down both edges of the tear, applying pressure for a short time. Clean off any surplus adhesive.

wood finishes

Stains and wood dyes in light and medium oak, mahogany and walnut can be used as wood finishes. Varnishes and sealers, such as oil or clear varnish with polyurethane sealers and wax type polishes are excellent for hardwoods. Perhaps the finest finish for smoothness and gloss is French polishing, a very skilled job which requires much patience. You can buy a French polishing kit with instructions or make up the solution yourself. The principal ingredient is shellac which is dissolved in methylated spirits, 6 oz. shellac to 1 pt. spirits. (You can buy this made up.) The process consists of applying a film of shellac to the wood surface and bringing the film up to a high gloss finish. Terms and stages are as follows: *Staining* the wood to darken. *Sealing* with polish. *Filling* the grain. *Fadding*, which is building up a good film of shellac for bodying up. *Colouring* (not always necessary) consists of touching in patches with the general tone. *Bodying-up* which is building up the final film of polish with small circular movements with the polish.
Finishing – there are one or two methods. In that described below, a rubber is charged with half polish and half spirit with no oil, the rubber moving over the work in straight strokes – backwards and forwards, one overlapping the other.

1 Before using the French polish cut a groove in a cork for application to the rubber to prevent too much pouring out at one time.

2 Clean up the work and sand smooth. Apply stain with a clean rag using quick strokes along the grain. Keep each edge wet for the next layer. Allow to dry for several hours.

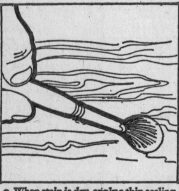

3 When stain is dry, apply a thin sealing coat of French polish. You can use a mop brush for this.

4 Fill the open grain to produce perfect surface. Filler can be superfine white plaster applied with a rag damped in clean water. Sand off with fine paper. Add a little oil to kill the whiteness.

5 Begin 'fadding' using a piece of material soaked in polish. Let material air harden for some time then soften in spirit. Dip again in polish and apply to wood in long strokes.

6 To make the rubber a piece of wadding about 9 in. square is folded as shown.

126

The four corners of the wadding are now lifted into a pyramid shape.

8 Cover the wadding with a clean piece of linen and flatten the sole of the rubber as shown.

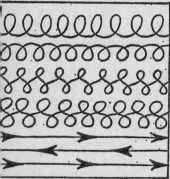

Complete 'fadding' using rubber without oil. Use circular movement as 1, then movement as 2. Finally long straight strokes as 3. There should be a good film on the work.

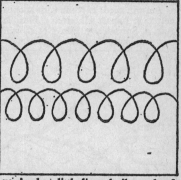

10 Apply a little linseed oil to sole of rubber and use strokes as shown to cover whole surface. Use flour grade glass paper to remove any ridges and continue strokes.

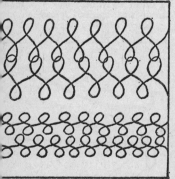

As body of polish builds up, change direction of strokes, using large and small. Keep rubber moving. Finish with long straight strokes.

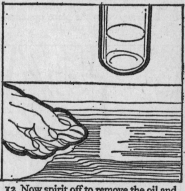

12 Now spirit off to remove the oil and get a good gloss. Charge a new rubber with half polish and half spirit. Work in circles first, then straight strokes.

For an egg-shell finish use a very fine steel wool and wax furniture polish. Dip wool in wax and work in long straight sweeps with the grain. Clean off surplus with clean rag.

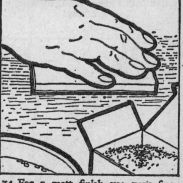

14 For a matt finish use very fine pumice powder on a felt pad damped with water. Apply long straight sweeps over work to cut down the French polish. Allow to dry. Rub over with a clean rag.

surfacing with laminate

Laminated table tops and worktops are decorative and durable. Once bonded to surface, laminate stands a great deal of rough treatment and still maintains its newnes. To cover a table top:

1 You will need: *1*. Knife with hooked cutter. *2*. Impact adhesive. *3*. Flexible rule. *4*. Spreader. *5*. File. Not shown: Laminate, Methylated spirits.

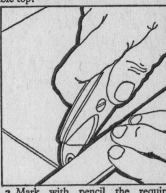

2 Mark with pencil the require measurements. With hooked cutt against straight edge cut along th pencil lines into the laminate.

3 Cut through half the thickness of the laminate. Snap the piece upwards completing the cut.

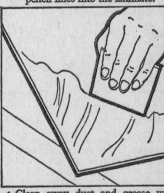

4 Clean away dust and grease wi methylated spirits. Spread an eve film of adhesive over the surface.

5 Coat table top surface similarly. Leave both surfaces about 10 minutes to get tacky.

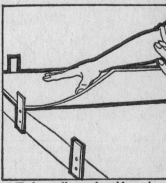

6 Tack small wood guide strips the side of the table to ensure squar ness. Press the laminate firmly dow

7 Finish flush all edges with a fine file. Don't chip the face of the laminate.

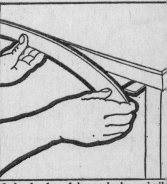

8 Apply the edging strip in a simila manner using guide strips below th table.

treatment of woodworm

Flight holes and wood dust show that your house has infested timbers which can cause deterioration and devaluation of your property. If the damage is extensive call in experts who will give you a free survey and deal with the trouble. For small areas and with the right equipment you can tackle it yourself. You can hire a pressure spray from your local builders or hire firms.

WARNING: *The spray fluids are very pungent so wear a light protective mask and very old clothing. Keep the fluid away from your skin. The chemical also affects polystyrene and rubber, so electric cables should be covered with polythene sheeting before spraying. Also should you have to spray near a water tank, cover it with a polythene sheet.*

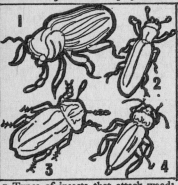

1 Types of insects that attack wood: *1.* Common furniture beetle. *2.* Lyctus beetle. *3.* Death-watch beetle. *4.* Long-horn beetle.

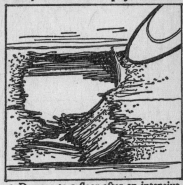

2 Damage to a floor after an intensive attack by woodworm.

3 You will need: *1.* Vacuum cleaner. *2.* Pressure spray. *3.* Aerosol injector. *4.* Can of woodworm fluid.

4 Remove all furniture from the room. Raise the floorboards that have become affected. These have flight holes and wood dust.

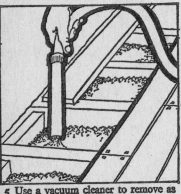

5 Use a vacuum cleaner to remove as much debris and dust as you can from between joists.

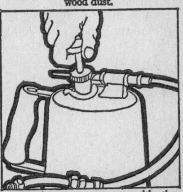

6 Fill the pressure spray with the chemical fluid and pump to the required pressure.

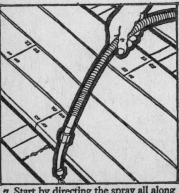

7 Start by directing the spray all along the joists and under the floorboards.

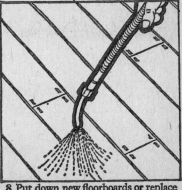

8 Put down new floorboards or replace old treated ones. Spray all over the surface of the boards, open windows, and leave for 48 hours.

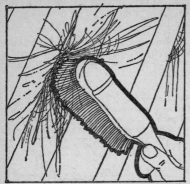

9 For infestation in the loft, brush all dust and cobwebs and generally make clean.

10 Use the spray and cover the whole of the timber so that it soaks well in. Don't miss any spots. Spray to retention.

11 Flight holes in furniture should be tackled immediately with an aerosol injector, injecting every hole.

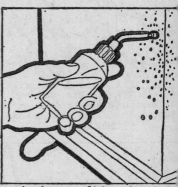

12 Another type of injector is a plastic press type with a rubber washer to make good contact with the edges of the holes.

recognition and treatment of timber decay

VIDENCE	LOCATION	CAUSE	TREATMENT
₅ in. diameter ₅und holes. ₅mall heaps of ₅ood dust.	On or below structural timbers and floorboards.	Exit holes of common furniture beetle.	Lift boards and spray. Spray structural timbers.
₅ in. diameter ₅und holes. ₅mall heaps of ₅ood dust.	On or under furniture.	Exit holes of common furniture beetle.	Inject woodworm fluid in holes or fumigate.
₅ in. diameter ₅les in oak or ₅rdwood. ₅mall heaps of ₅ood dust with ₅n-shaped pellets.	On or below structural timbers in old houses.	Exit holes of death watch beetle.	Call in timber preservation experts.
₅rge oval holes ₅casionally with ₅stered appearance ₅ surface of soft ₅ood.	Roofing and flooring timbers.	Exit holes of the house longhorn beetle.	Call in timber preservation experts immediately.
₅ in. round ₅les. ₅rge heaps of ₅wdered frass.	Hardwood flooring and panelling. Under flooring or furniture.	Exit holes of lyctus beetle.	Inject into flight holes and spray accessible surfaces.

Keeping the House Warm and Dry

causes and prevention of damp

Damp causes more damage and deterioration to a house than any other effect. It is important to recognise the different types of damp and apply the correct treatment. Surface treatment alone may turn out to be only a temporary measure and the damp will start again. Here are the signs to look for and certain remedies within the scope of the handyman.

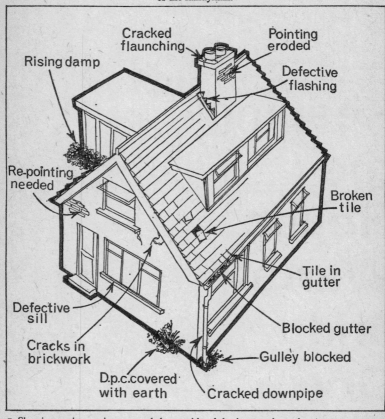

Cracked flaunching

Pointing eroded

Rising damp

Defective flashing

Re-pointing needed

Broken tile

Tile in gutter

Defective sill

Blocked gutter

Cracks in brickwork

Gulley blocked

D.p.c. covered with earth

Cracked downpipe

1 Showing various points around the outside of the house where damp can penetrate to the inside.

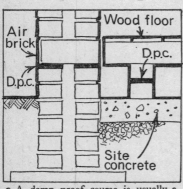

Air brick

Wood floor

D.p.c.

D.p.c.

Site concrete

2 A damp proof course is usually a horizontal layer of slate or PVC membrane. Many older types of houses were built without one.

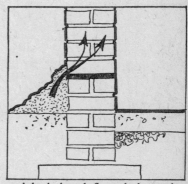

3 A banked earth flower bed near the wall of the house above the damp proof course provides a bridge for damp to enter. Remove banked earth.

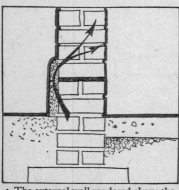

4 The external wall rendered above the dpc will form a path for the damp to rise. Cut back the rendering to below the dpc.

5 Mortar droppings in the bottom of a cavity wall have reached above the dpc and will allow access to damp. The builder should be called to clear it.

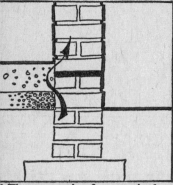

6 The concrete site of an extension has been built above the dpc. Damp can get through here as a bridge is formed.

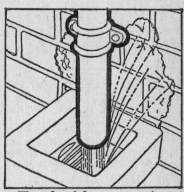

7 Water forced from a waste pipe or rain water thrown back above the dpc.

8 Fit a shoe to help delay the force of water and direct it away from the house wall.

9 A blocked up air vent stops the flow of air circulating under the house. Dry rot in the timbers can result.

10 Clear all plants and debris from the outside walls. Lower the earth around the house.

11 A cracked down pipe can cause the growth of green moss on the wall. Renew the pipe or effect a repair.

12 Treat brick surfaces with a damp repellant solution. This is a clear liquid and will not affect the colour of the bricks.

13 Debris blocking the outlet above a bay window. In heavy rain the water rises and penetrates below or ruptures roof covering. Clear this.

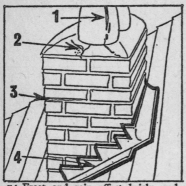

14 Frost and rain affect bricks and mortar. *1.* Cracked pot. *2.* Cracked flaunching. *3.* Bricks need repointing. *4.* Zinc flashing may have moved through defective pointing.

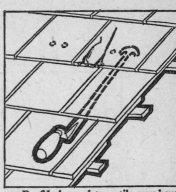

15 Roof leaks; a slate or tile may have slipped or cracked; slate nails may be corroded. Break off securing nails with 'ripper'.

16 Use a zinc strip about 1 in. by 2 in. longer than the slate. Nail or bend it over rafter batten.

17 Lay slate over the zinc strip. Push it under those above into the position of the damaged slate. Turn up the zinc strip to hold slate fast.

18 A fallen tile can get lodged in the gutter causing the rain water to flow over and down the wall.

19 The watershed can affect damp all down the wall. This must be attended to otherwise damp will penetrate.

20 Attend to loose gutter brackets. If necessary, to stop an overshoot, move the gutter out a little with small fillets of wood placed behind each bracket.

21 A cracked or broken hopper ca cause damp walls. Arrow points to ba joint where water percolates and rus gathers.

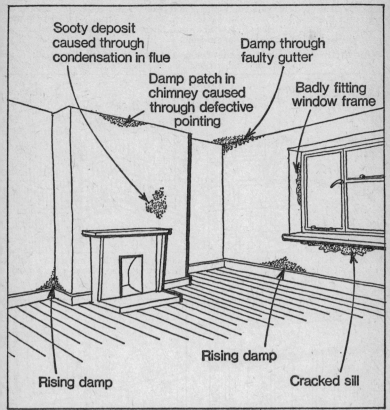

Sooty deposit caused through condensation in flue

Damp patch in chimney caused through defective pointing

Damp through faulty gutter

Badly fitting window frame

Rising damp

Rising damp

Cracked sill

22 Showing some of the defects inside a room resulting from faults previously mentioned on the outside of the house. Damp patches on walls can be treated by using metallic foil put up in a similar way to wallpapering. The roll of metalic foil is about 15 in. wide by 30 ft. long.

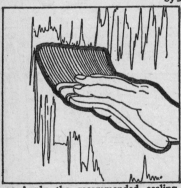

23 Apply the recommended sealing coat of water resistant adhesive to the whole wall and allow to dry.

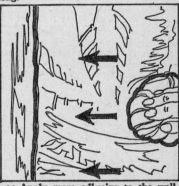

24 Apply more adhesive to the wall and hang the foil. Smooth at once because adhesive dries very quickly.

25 As foil unrolls, smooth with cloth to disperse air bubbles. If torn use adhesive again and cover tear with foil and 1 in. overlap.

26 Continue round the wall overlapping about 1 in. Wipe all adhesive off foil. Cover with lining paper, then wallpaper or paint.

Builders often use Newtonite lath, a pitch impregnated fibre formed into corrugated sheets supplied in 5 yard long rolls 1 yard wide. The lathing is nailed directly to the damp wall and corrugations are plastered over. Slight gaps at floor level provide a passage of air to circulate and dry out the damp.

WARNING: The new plastering must not have any contact with the damp walls, or a damp solid floor, otherwise all the work will be useless.

27 If you have one wall that is damp, remove all plaster down to the brick face.

28 Unroll the lath along the wall. Here it is being placed over a solid floor.

29 Methods of fixing *a*. drive clout nails into mortar joints, *b*. drive harden nails through metal strip into brick as far as the strip depresses.

30 With a solid floor, raise the lath to allow ventilation. There must be a slight gap under the skirting.

31 Above shows a timber floor with the lath lowered between wall and floor timbers.

32 Lath can be fixed horizontally. For a corner joint apply a bitumen felt strip to prevent the new plaster seeping on to the wet wall at the back.

33 Showing how a butt joint is protected by the bitumen felt strip.

34 A light first coat of plaster just fills the grooves. Finish with a hard wall plaster. Allow a good drying out period before decorating.

condensation and its treatment

Condensation occurs in most houses, caused by moisture vapour which varies according to the climatic conditions on the outside, as well as the effect of steam from kitchens and bathrooms. The remedy is to have adequate ventilation, an even room temperature and the insulation of cold walls and windows.

1 This shows the effect when warm, moist air meets a cold surface and releases its moisture as condensation. Rivulets of water drip down paintwork and fittings.

2 Use expanded polystyrene to combat condensation. Hang it like wallpaper using the correct adhesive.

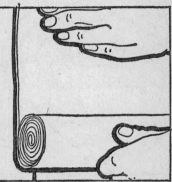

3 Plumb line the wall and fit each length. Overlap the polystyrene by about ½ in.

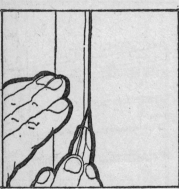

4 Using a straight edge trim off carefully with a sharp knife to get a perfect butt joint.

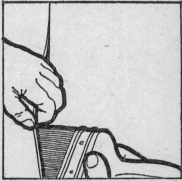

5 Lift the edge of the polystyrene and brush adhesive under the raised edge. Roll back firmly into position.

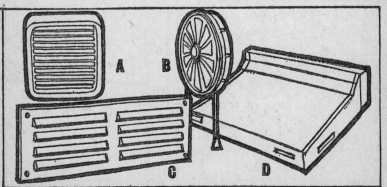

6 A few appliances that will help reduce condensation in the home. A. louvre shutter extractor fan. B. Self-actuating ventilating unit. C. Louvre type ventilator. D. A cooker hood to disperse cooking smells. Some types will take the smell and steam through ducts to the outside air.

fit an extractor fan

An extractor fan in a window frame can be fitted in quite a short time. Here's how to fit one type of extractor. These instructions apply to many others on the market. Some types, however, are fitted through the kitchen wall. You will need a circular glass cutter which can be hired, a glass cutter, a hammer and pincers. Always follow the makers' instructions when wiring the fan. YOU MUST HAVE A CORRECTLY RATED FLEXIBLE CORD CONNECTED TO IT.

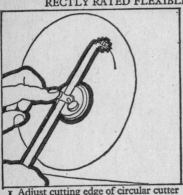

1 Adjust cutting edge of circular cutter to required radius. Attach sucker and score first circle with even pressure. Move cutter in about ⅜ in. and score second circle.

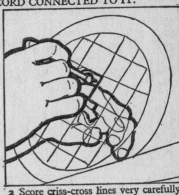

2 Score criss-cross lines very carefully in the inner circle with glass cutter. Tap out each small portion of glass.

3 You should easily be able to lift out the remaining segments of glass.

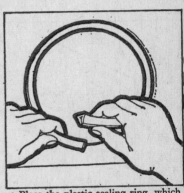

4 Place the plastic sealing ring, which has a channel on the outside, into the hole.

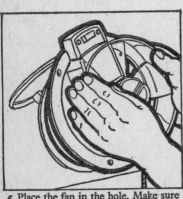

5 Place the fan in the hole. Make sure the plastic ribs on the top side fit over the plastic ring.

6 Lift up the fan and fit the bottom ribs over the edge of the plastic ring. Pull down the fan so that the bottom touches the ring.

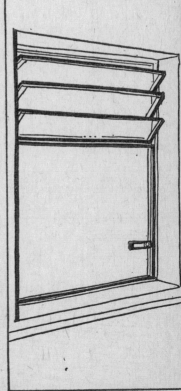

7 Louvre windows will greatly help to get rid of moist air when open, and will keep out the rain.

airlocks in a radiator

Air tends to collect at the top of radiators. This is why air vent valves are provided. If a radiator does not warm up properly it is probably due to air collecting and forming a lock in the system. You will have to bleed the system by opening the valve. Should you get frequent air locks you can obtain an automatic air valve to fit your existing radiator.

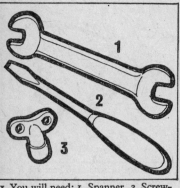

1 You will need: *1*. Spanner. *2*. Screwdriver. *3*. Radiator key.

2 To clear an air lock apply the key to the air vent and open. When all the air has escaped close the vent. Catch any water in a jar.

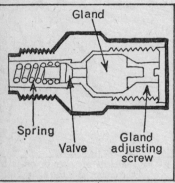

Gland

Spring

Valve

Gland adjusting screw

3 Here is an automatic air valve which will allow the air to escape but not the water.

4 If you often get an air lock, install this type of air valve. Start by draining the system.

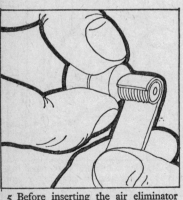

5 Before inserting the air eliminator valve cover the threaded portion with a plastic tape to make a waterproof joint.

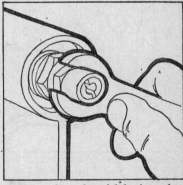

6 Screw the valve tightly into the radiator.

7 Now fill the system. With a screwdriver unscrew the adjustment to release a quantity of air.

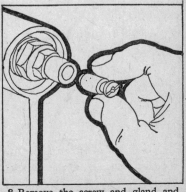

8 Remove the screw and gland and depress the valve to bleed off, then screw back.

sealing those cracks

Cracks will develop at certain points in a house, however well it is built, and moisture and damp will penetrate if these are not attended to. The use of caulking compound – sold with a gun or tube for application – is an effective remedy. Apply mortar or cellulose filler first if cracks are wider than ⅜ in.

1 This is a pressure gun being loaded with a cartridge of sealant. There are many different types which you can buy or hire.

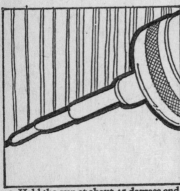

2 Hold the gun at about 45 degrees and run it along a crevice getting a good fillet.

3 Use sufficient pressure in order to fill the cracks with the mastic.

4 In small places where use of the gun is difficult, use a portion of coiled mastic, and press home with your fingers.

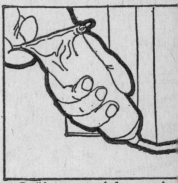

5 Caulking compound also comes in a tube which you squeeze by rolling from the bottom.

6 Sealing round a door frame will keep out dust and dirt.

7 Apply sealing compound between window frames and the brickwork.

8 Sealant applied to the base of brick where it meets masonry.

9 For cracks in outside waste pipes. Seal all around the joint.

10 Cracks often occur at the base of steps. Fill large cracks with mortar first, then apply the sealant.

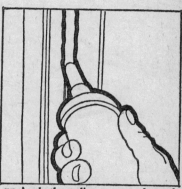

11 Apply the sealing compound round door frames that have warped.

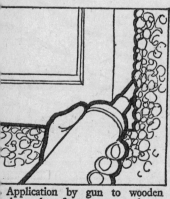

12 Application by gun to wooden windows where frame meets rough cast walling.

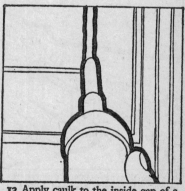

13 Apply caulk to the inside gap of a window. Make a smooth fillet and after a few days paint over it.

14 Underneath a window ledge is a vulnerable place for cracks.

15 Gaps occur at the top of French windows. Seal all round the top frames to prevent any dirt getting in.

closing that gap

In many houses unsightly and draughty gaps, often caused by shrinking and subsidence, appear under skirting boards. Use quadrant moulding to deal with this and seal the room from draughts.

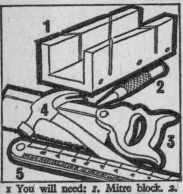

1 You will need: *1.* Mitre block. *2.* Nail punch. *3.* Tenon saw. *4.* Hammer. *5.* Flexible rule. Not shown: Pins, Glue, Wood Filler, Nails.

2 Examples of some of the mouldings to be obtained in 6 ft. to 8 ft. lengths from most timber merchants.

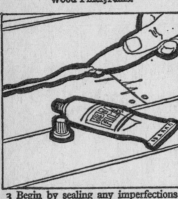

3 Begin by sealing any imperfections or holes in the skirting board with either plastic or wood filler.

4 Measure the lengths of moulding required and mark off with a pencil.

5 Using the mitre board cut the required length, with one end mitred at an angle of 45°.

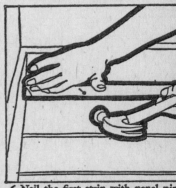

6 Nail the first strip with panel pin at 6 in. to 8 in. intervals. Always nail into the floorboards.

·7 The next strip should be mitred at right angles for the corners.

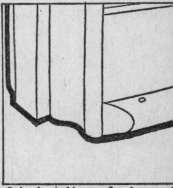

8 At the architrave of a door, angle back the moulding, rounding smooth to prevent sharp edges.

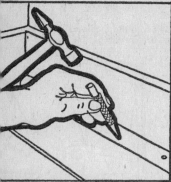

Punch all pins below the surface with a nail punch. Fill the holes in the mouldings with wood filler to conceal.

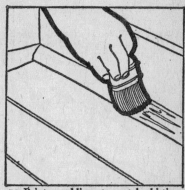

10 Paint mouldings to match skirting board.

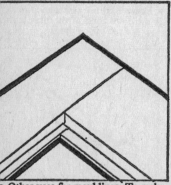

Other uses for mouldings. To make neat job of a glass door, a quadrant looks much better than putty.

moulding

glass putty

12 Measure and mitre the moulding. Seat the glass on the putty as shown. Pin the moulding to the frame.

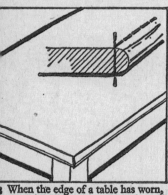

When the edge of a table has worn, w a straight line as shown, cutting off the old wood.

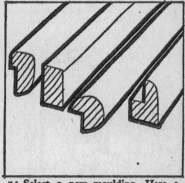

14 Select a new moulding. Here a hardwood rectangular section is shown.

Apply a good impact glue to the ge of the table and to the moulding. Leave both for about ten minutes.

16 Press the moulding into position. Panel pin for extra strength at intervals. Punch with nail punch and fill up holes with filler.

blocking up a fireplace

Many people these days have turned away from the open fire. An empty fireplace looks rather forlorn. One way to brighten its appearance is to block it in with peg board. It is advisable to have the chimney swept before you start this job and to make good any cracks inside the fireplace.

NOTE: We have used a fire-proof cement in case at some time you wish to return to an open fire.

WARNING: You must always provide ventilation to the fireplace. Peg board or a small ventilator would be suitable and will prevent damp in the chimney.

1 You will need: *1.* Screwdriver. *2.* Trowel. *3.* Tin of fireproof cement. *4.* Paint brush. *5.* Old brush. *6.* Mallet.

2 Remove the fire basket and fire front. If these are fixed to the hearth chisel them out.

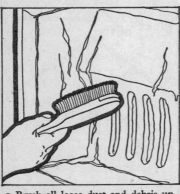

3 Brush all loose dust and debris up. Rake out the cracks with a trowel.

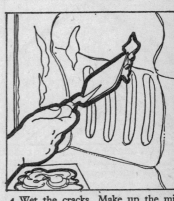

4 Wet the cracks. Make up the mix and apply with a trowel. Also smooth off the hearth if necessary.

5 Measure width and depth of opening and cut 2 in. x 1 in. timber to size. Put side members up first and wedge top and bottom ones to make tight fit.

6 Cut the peg board to the exact size of the outer edges of the wooden frame width and depth.

7 Using 1 in. screws, drive these home at intervals round the frame.

8 Give the peg board two coats of paint.

save warmth by insulation

Insulation will keep the whole house comfortably warm. Without it 30–40 per cent of the heat produced by an effective heating system can be lost. You will save enormously on fuel costs by insulating the roof space, eliminating draughts, and lagging pipes.

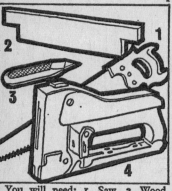

1 You will need: 1. Saw. 2. Wood spreader. 3. Cutting knife. 4. Stapler.

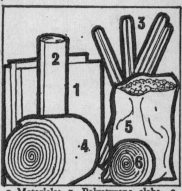

2 Materials: 1. Polystyrene slabs. 2. Aluminium foil. 3. Foam rubber sleeves. 4. Mineral wool blanket. 5. Vermiculite granules. 6. Roll of felt Bandage.

3 Pour vermiculite granules straight from bag in between joists for good insulation.

4 Use a home-made spreader to even out the granules. Cover all pipes to a depth of about 2 in.

5 Roll a 2 in. thick fibre-glass or mineral wool blanket between joists.

6 Tack aluminium foil to the joists or rafters in the attic. Lay its flat face uppermost and its serrated side underneath.

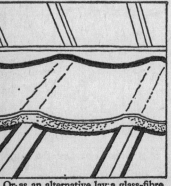

7 Or as an alternative lay a glass-fibre quilt across the joists.

8 Lag the tank with square cut pieces of expanded polystyrene fitted to make a box.

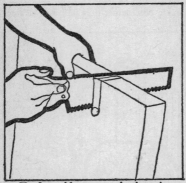

9 To fit a side over projecting pipes, drill holes in the square coinciding with the pipe projection. Saw slot down to hole.

10 Save the off-cut of polystyrene to slot back after the sides have been joined round the tank.

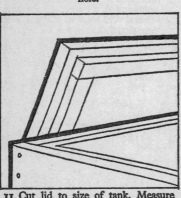

11 Cut lid to size of tank. Measure strips, or off-cuts of polystyrene to form a ledge. This will fit into the tank as shown.

12 Lag all pipes with a bandage of felt. Allow each turn of felt to overlap the next turn.

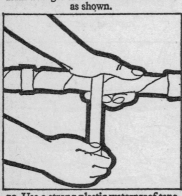

13 Use a strong plastic waterproof tape to secure the bandage. Tape the felt bandage at intervals.

14 Over certain joints and valves secure the bandage with strong string or twine.

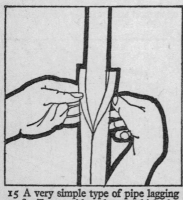

15 A very simple type of pipe lagging to fit. Foam rubber sleeves which slot over pipes.

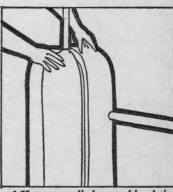

16 Hot water cylinders need insulating to conserve heat. Use sections of mineral fibre quilting.

Use band fittings to hold the quilting in position.

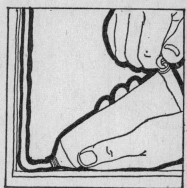
18 This is a mastic-type draught excluder which hardens after application. Squeeze on from tube.

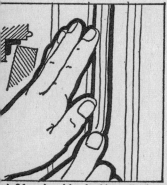
A felt strip with a backing adhesive is very suitable for door insulation.

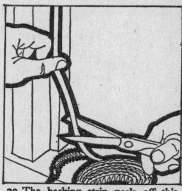
20 The backing strip peels off this self adhesive draught proofing strip.

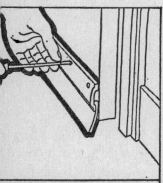
Fit a plastic and rubber door bottom seal to stop draughts at floor level.

22 A floor draught excluder fitted with a flexible rubber moulding screwed to the floor.

A roll-on thin polystyrene ceiling veer can also be used for walls prior wallpapering; has good thermal qualities.

24 Decorative polystyrene tiles are easy to fit to a ceiling for good insulation.

Outdoor Jobs

cold asphalt and other paths

Here we show you how to lay a cold asphalt path. The black or brown asphalt com[...] in hundredweight bags. Stone chips are supplied with the purchase.

1 Remove all weeds in a soil or gravel foundation and compact it with a roller. Concrete must be treated with cold bitumen primer for easy spreading.

2 Open the bag of cold asphalt. Loose[...] the contents with a spade to hel[...] spreading.

3 Spread the asphalt with a rake to an even depth of about ¾ in. Check occasionally for level.

4 Now roll the surface with a garde[...] roller. In warm weather wet the roll[...] to prevent it sticking.

5 Scatter the stone chips evenly over the path. Roll once more, keeping the roller wet to prevent it picking up the chips.

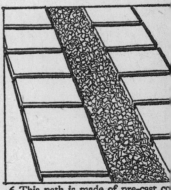

6 This path is made of pre-cast co[...] crete slabs laid on a bed of mortar w[...] loose laid flintstones in the cent[...]

7 Stepping stones of pre-cast concrete in a lawn. Cut squares of turf out of the lawn and bed the stones on a 1½-2 in. bed of sand.

8 Lay attractive multi-coloured cr[...] paving on foundation of 3-4 in. clin[...] or hardcore and 2 in. mortar. Sma[...] stones in centre. Shape mortar alo[...] edge of each stone with trowel. Ch[...] level of path.

making a brick path

You can make a very attractive path with cheap bricks which you can often get second-hand from a builder's yard. Make many patterns for your path as shown below. Remember to level the ground and use pegs and lines. Always use a spirit level.

1 Lay your bricks on a dry foundation of weak sand/cement levelled to about 3 in. deep. Allow about ½ in. joint gap between.

2 An attractive herringbone pattern. The angle at the edges can be filled with cement or you can cut angled bricks.

3 For edging bricks, lay them on a bed of wet mortar along a string line. Provide an angled slope on the outside.

4 Spread a dry mix over the bricks. Be careful not to move any of them as you do this.

5 Sweep the dry mix over the bricks and into the joints, making sure each joint is filled.

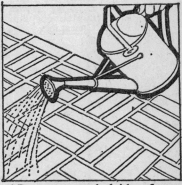

6 Pour water over the brick surface to wet the bedding and joints until joints are filled. Brush off all cement on bricks.

7 Interpose concrete slabs with a brick pattern for a very attractive path.

8 A circle of bricks around an ornament, perhaps a sundial, can add an interesting corner to your garden.

153

laying a concrete walk

A well laid concrete path between a lawn or flowerbeds needs the minimum of upkeep. The first step in making the path is to prepare a good solid soil base. This should be rolled and levelled with gravel or cinders.

WARNING: Do not lay concrete in frosty weather. Don't use too much water in the mixture: this will weaken it and lead to surface cracks when the concrete hardens. Too little water results in air holes or 'honeycombing'.

2 Mix on a hard surface one bucket cement, 2 buckets of sand and 3 buckets of gravel.

3 Thoroughly mix the sand, cement and gravel together.

1 You will need: *1.* Bucket. *2.* Shovel. *3.* Level. *4.* Steel trowel. *5.* Saw. *6.* Hammer. *7.* Timber for frame. *8.* Wood Float. *9.* Edging Trowel. *10.* Steel Rule. *11.* Measuring Box. Not shown: Cement mix.

4 Add ¾ bucket of water and mix to an even consistency.

5 Determine the line for the formwork and set 2 in. × 2 in. pegs at about 6 ft. intervals. Nail the timber to the pegs.

6 At 4 ft. intervals partition the forms with strips at right angles to the sides. Work alternate sections when filling with concrete.

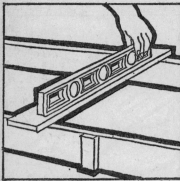

7 Use the level to check all stages of the formwork. Level the ground in between to allow a shallow bed of sand or fine ashes about 2 in. deep.

8 Wet the formwork. Spade the concrete in alternate sections. Allow it to rise about ½ in. above formwork.

9 Screed off top of concrete with a sawing and chopping action. After alternate sections harden remove cross strips. Fill remainder. Screed. Cover each area with polythene sheeting.

10 When the concrete has stiffened smooth with a wood float. Use the edging trowel between the sections and edges of the path.

11 For a textured look on the surface brush the concrete with a soft broom about an hour after laying the concrete.

12 For a cobble stone finish, bed stones in mortar on a 3 in. concrete base. The mortar mix is 1 part cement to 3 parts sharp sand. Level.

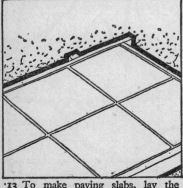

13 To make paving slabs, lay the concrete in formwork on ½ in. sand. When stiff measure and cut rectangles with pointing trowel. Leave three days.

14 Make string lines. Lay slabs on a mortar mix 1 in. thick with joints ½ in. apart. Check level. Tap each slab into place. Fill joints with sand or a dry mix mortar placed ¼ in. below the surface and watered in.

simple bricklaying

Simple bricklaying is within the scope of most amateurs. A 4½ in. or 9 in. wall will be serviceable in a garden but must have a solid foundation. The concrete foundation should be wider than the brickwork and not less than 12 in. below ground level. The trench should be dug out to lines and pegs inserted in the middle, so that the tops of the pegs are the correct level for the finished concrete.

1 You will need: *1.* Bolster chisel. *2.* Brick trowel. *3.* Pointing trowel. *4.* Spirit level. *5.* Piece of piping or pointing tool. *6.* Length of string. *7.* Hawk. *8.* Hammer.

2 Check foundation is level. Lay some bricks at the corner of each end to fix a string line.

3 Check vertical and horizontal lines with spirit level. Apply corner leads attached to a small nail in mortar joint.

4 Place mortar for bed joint. Recess middle of the bed with point of trowel.

5 Slap a good dab of mortar on the end of the brick to be layed.

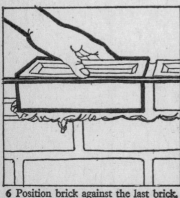

6 Position brick against the last brick. If too high, tap it down until level.

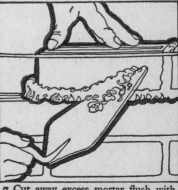

7 Cut away excess mortar flush with the brick. Always draw the trowel towards you.

8 Keep checking level of work.

9 For a two-tier wall, work the mortar between the centre joint of each course.

10 Lay a finished header course on a good mortar bed, tap into position and use level.

11 With a small pipe, compress the mortar into a concave slope over mortar joints. This is 'tooling.'

12 Leave to set for a few days. Then brush the wall to remove loose particles of mortar.

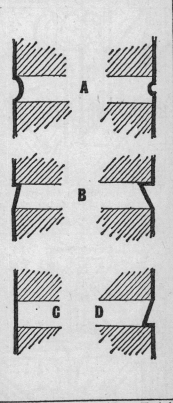

14 Some types of pointing: *a.* Tooled joints. *b.* Weathered pointing. *c.* Flush joint. *d.* Struck joint.

13 Use a Bolster chisel to cut bricks for small spaces. Hammer, with sharp taps.

building an open screen wall

Open screen walling makes an attractive addition to your house and garden and provides a pleasant screen. You can choose from different designs. Slotted pilaster blocks in white or coloured cement are used to provide stability for the patterned wall.

1 Prepare a firm foundation. Mark out position of footings with pegs and string. Dig a shallow trench about 9 in. deep. Put wooden pegs 3 ft. apart. Set level.

2 Fill the trench with concrete mix 1 part cement, 2½ parts sand and 4 parts coarse aggregate by volume. Compact level to top of pegs and allow to set.

3 Place pilaster blocks at a maximum of 10 ft. apart. Place first two and line up by stringing. Check for level and plumb for vertical. Lay first course on mix, 3 parts sand, 1 part cement.

4 Spread mortar on edge of block and base to mate up with the first one laid. Continue until first course is finished.

5 Check periodically with spirit level to see that the blocks are true vertically.

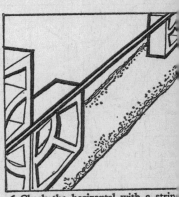

6 Check the horizontal with a string line stretched between the tops of the end blocks of each row.

7 Blocks should be tapped carefully into alignment on their mortar beds. Do not lay too many courses at one time.

8 Allow about 10 minutes for the mortar to stiffen. Clean up with an old brush.

building a simple fence

A fence is usually needed as a boundary line to your property and can be an expensive outlay. Make your own simple fence – your only expense will be the cost of materials.

1 Fix a taut line to work to between corner posts (other posts can follow in between). Dig a hole about 2 ft. deep by 1 ft. square.

2 Fill the bottom of the hole with about 3 in. of gravel for drainage and prepare the concrete mix.

3 Pre-treat the post with chemical preservative and sink it on to the gravel base. Fill with concrete. Brace the post with temporary stakes.

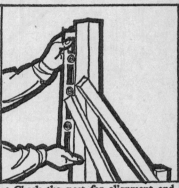

4 Check the post for alignment and correct height. Adjust if necessary.

5 Tamp down the concrete. Put a collar or slope of concrete about ground level to help to drain away any rainwater. Leave to set for a few days.

6 Put in the remaining posts. Add a top rail. Nail with galvanized nails and check horizontal with level.

7 Should a second rail be needed, some of the simple joints you can make are shown above.

8 To get correct alignment for a second rail, measure carefully down each post and join. Fence can then be filled in with boards or panels.

repairs to fences

Bad weather in winter will cause fractures and damp rot in fences. Should this happen to yours, don't immediately think about a new fence. It's simple to repair a fence well enough to last for many more years.

1 This post is affected by damp and has rotted away at the base, but the upper part is sound.

2 Dig a hole for a concrete spur about 15 in. square by 2ft. deep. Remove the rotted part of the stump.

3 Place the spur in position. Lightly hammer screw bolts into the post to mark position, remove spur and drill about ½ in. into marks.

4 Place the spur back into position and screw home the bolts with a spanner.

5 Check with a spirit level to see that the post is true vertically.

6 Compact some hardcore at the base of the hole by tamping.

8 Prepare a stiff mix from 5 parts sand and ballast to 1 of cement. Ram the mix into the hole.

7 Check the vertical with the spirit level again. Nail a temporary strut with a stake as shown.

9 Prepare a concrete collar above ground level and angle down as shown. Allow to set for 2 to 3 days before removing temporary frame.

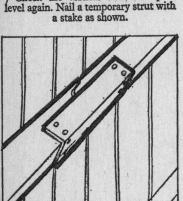

10 Repair a fractured arris rail with a metal angle bracket placed over the split and screwed to either side.

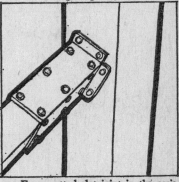

11 For a rotted slot joint in the arris rail, saw the part off cleanly and attach a galvanised metal bracket as shown.

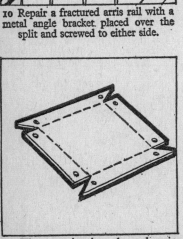

12 Water seeping into the end grain often rots the tops of fence posts. Protect the top with a zinc cap. Cut a shape to the post size.

13 Tap the sides of the cap down over the post. Tuck the triangular shapes under the outer two sides. Secure with galvanised nails.

constructing a fence in pvc

This type of fencing is made of tough PVC. There are no parts to rust or rot and it does not need painting. Only an occasional washing over with detergent is necessary. It is very simple to fit as shown below and will look attractive in any garden.

1 Measure the required height of post. Cut the number you require with a fine toothed saw.

2 Assemble a number of posts together and carefully mark the plank positions on each.

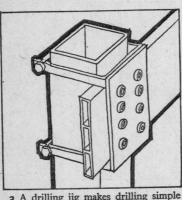

3 A drilling jig makes drilling simple and accurate. You can obtain this with the sections of PVC.

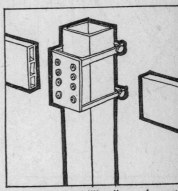

4 Position the drilling jig on the post

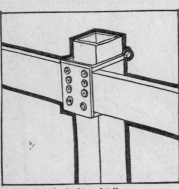

5 Fit the planks into the jig.

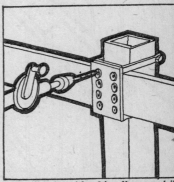

6 Drill holes with a $\frac{3}{8}$ in. diameter dril for the planks that butt, drill top an bottom of each plank. For plank passing through post drill top right an bottom left holes.

7 Remove jig and insert fixing plug barrels into the holes until they snap on.

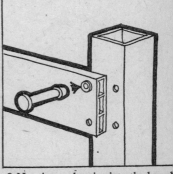

8 Now insert the pins into the barrel until they snap home.

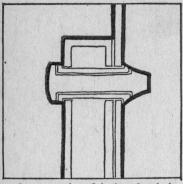

9 A cross section of the barrel and pin locked in position.

10 Construct the first section of fence. Best to work on the ground.

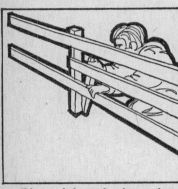

11 Dig post holes to the plan you have made. Provide a temporary holding stake.

12 Continue to build successive sections until completed.

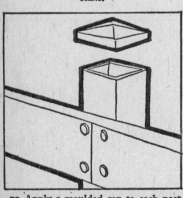

13 Apply a moulded cap to each post using a solvent weld cement.

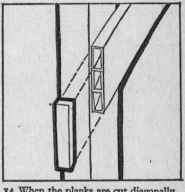

14 When the planks are cut diagonally you will have to use strip capping.

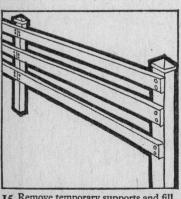

15 Remove temporary supports and fill in the holes with a good concrete mix. Allow to set firm.

16 A gate for your fence. Post is plugged with a timber block to support the gate and take the hinges.

Plumbing

frozen pipes

If a plumber is not available when you have a frozen or split pipe, you can deal with this yourself if you follow the instructions below.

WARNING: DO NOT USE A BLOW LAMP, IT CAN CAUSE A FIRE IF NOT USED PROPERLY.

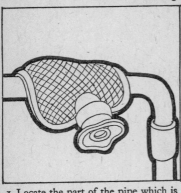

1 Locate the part of the pipe which is frozen and cover with hot water bottles or hot cloths.

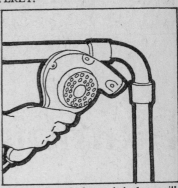

2 The warm air from a hair dryer will give a slow continuous heat and should thaw out the pipe quickly.

3 In conditions of extreme cold, a sink waste pipe may freeze up. Pouring salt down the waste and placing hot cloths on the 'U' bend beneath it should help to unfreeze the pipe.

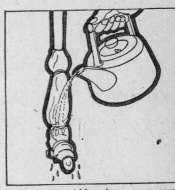

4 For an outside pipe, wrap some heavy rags round the frozen part, and pour on boiling water.

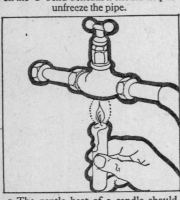

5 The gentle heat of a candle should thaw a frozen stopcock in time. Keep the candle away from any combustible material.

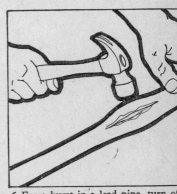

6 For a burst in a lead pipe, turn off the main supply, place a bowl under the pipe and gently tap the split until closed.

7 Thoroughly dry the pipe with a cloth. With an old knife scrape the lead clean round the burst. Rough up lightly with a file to give key for bandage.

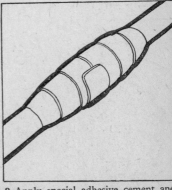

8 Apply special adhesive cement and wrapping in accordance with the makers' instructions and allow to set.

leaking overflow

When the overflow pipe of a W.C. cistern delivers a steady drip or flow of water, this usually means trouble with the ball valve or a punctured float. The fault could be a worn washer, grit in the valve seating, or that the copper float has worn very thin. If it is the float then a replacement plastic ball is all that will be needed. Replacement of a new valve washer is shown below. For clarity of illustration, the siphon chamber has been omitted.

WARNING: Turn OFF the water supply before beginning.

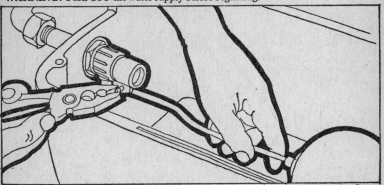

1 Turn off the water supply to the cistern. Lift the cover and put it on the floor. Holding the ball arm with one hand extract the split-pin with pliers.

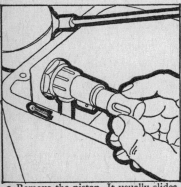

2 Remove the piston. It usually slides out easily, but if stubborn use a small ·screwdriver through the slot to lever it out.

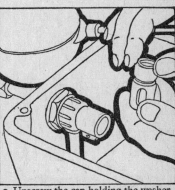

3 Unscrew the cap holding the washer. If it is stiff use pliers. Take care not to damage cylinder.

4 Remove worn washer. Clean and grease valve components. Grit particles can prevent seating. Put on new washer, insert piston, clean split pin and reassemble.

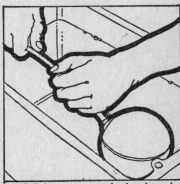

5 If slight wear occurs in the pivot pin and bearing, bend the ball arm downwards.

6 To make a punctured ball work until it can be replaced, drain the ball and enclose it in a strong plastic bag.

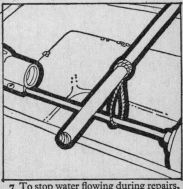

7 To stop water flowing during repairs, tie the arm to a wooden cross-piece.

unblocking a wastepipe

Basins, baths and sinks often become blocked with too much waste. Try flushing the sink with boiling water and common soda. If this is unsuccessful there are alternative methods to use.

1 You will need: *1*. Plunger. *2*. Wrench. *3*. Screwdriver. *4*. Flexible Curtain wire. *5*. Cloth. *6*. Petroleum Jelly.

2 Try the plunger first. Plug the overflow hole with a cloth to obtain full pressure.

3 Part fill the basin. Grease plunger rim to help suction. Place plunger over waste hole. Work handle vigorously up and down. Remove plunger.

4 If blockage is dislodged, the water will drain away. Run fresh water for short time.

5 If the water empties slowly or not at all, blockage could be in the U trap. Turn a flexible wire slowly.

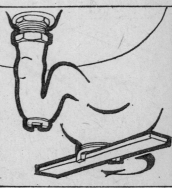

6 Place bucket under the U bend. Unscrew the plug using a small block of wood locked in the lugs.

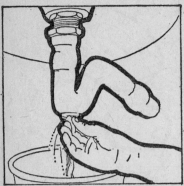

7 All waste should fall out as plug is released. Pieces can be pulled out by hand.

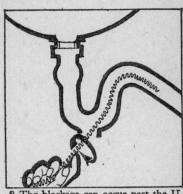

8 The blockage can occur past the U bend. Use the wire again and twist until the blockage is freed.

9 Lavatory blockages can be dislodged by using the wire in the same way.

10 As well as twisting the wire you may have to jerk out pieces of tissue.

11 Make a home-made plunger with a mop head.

12 Wrap the mop in a strong plastic bag. Tie it tightly round the mop handle with string. Use the mop as a force pump.

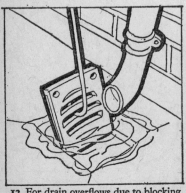

13 For drain overflows due to blocking by leaves, earth and tealeaves. Start by lifting the grating.

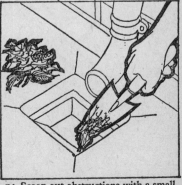

14 Scoop out obstructions with a small trowel. Flush with disinfectant. Replace the grating.

replacing a tap washer

A dripping tap is not only an annoyance. It also causes corrosion and wastes water. Nine times out of ten you will find that the trouble is a faulty washer.

WARNING: The water must be turned off at the MAIN STOP VALVE before starting this job.

1 If a tap drips continually, see if the old washer is worn, and if so, fit a new washer of the correct size.

2 You will need a ½ in. washer for sinks or basins and ¾ in. washer for bath or mixer taps.

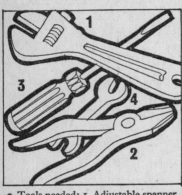

3 Tools needed: *1*. Adjustable spanner. *2*. Pliers. *3*. Screwdriver. *4*. Small spanner.

4 Turn off the stop valve. This is usually under the sink. Turn on the tap until the water stops running.

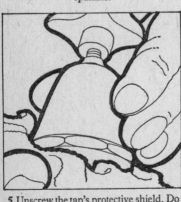

5 Unscrew the tap's protective shield. Do this carefully to avoid damaging the chrome finish.

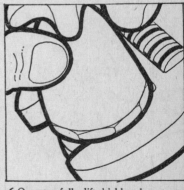

6 Open tap fully, lift shield and unscrew the hexagon nut with the adjustable spanner. Lift the tap from its seat.

7 Remove the jumper which rests loosely in the tap base. The washer and the jumper are held together with a nut.

In a hot tap the jumper is pinned to the tap head and cannot be removed.

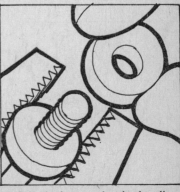

8 Grip the jumper plate in the pliers and undo the nut with the small spanner. Remove the old washer and fit a new one. Put the tap together and test for drip.

9 This shows a pull off head type of modern tap which simplifies getting to the inside.

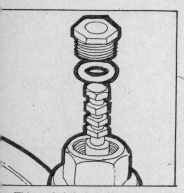

10 This exploded view shows the main spindle and gland nut with plastic 'O' ring.

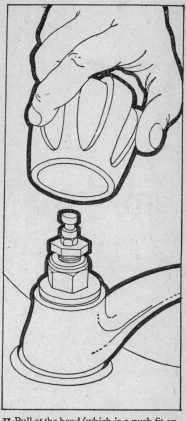

11 Pull at the head (which is a push fit on the spindle) firmly, to reveal the gland nut.

12 A drip coming from the base of the swivel nozzle shows that the washer is worn. Turn off the mains tap and undo the shoulder shroud.

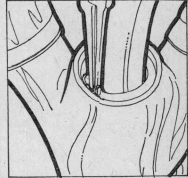

13 Revealed is a copper retaining circlip fitted with an annular groove. Spring this out with a pair of pliers.

14 Lift nozzle clear. Pull out worn washer (or washers) and fit new ones. Moisten the neoprene rings on the bottom of the nozzle when re-assembling.

changing a
supatap washer

It is unnecessary to turn off the main water supply when changing a supatap washer because the body contains a check valve which automatically stops the flow.

1 If water is dripping constantly from the tap a replacement washer is needed.

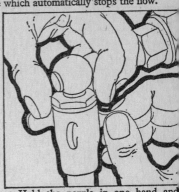

2 Hold the nozzle in one hand and loosen the gland nut with your fingers or with a spanner.

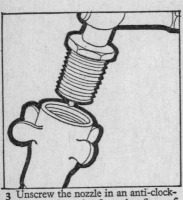

3 Unscrew the nozzle in an anti-clockwise direction. At first the flow of water will increase, but will stop as the check valve falls into position.

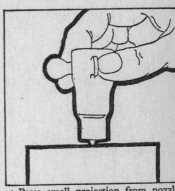

4 Press small projection from nozzle against a hard surface to release it.

5 Turn the nozzle upside down and the anti-splash will fall out.

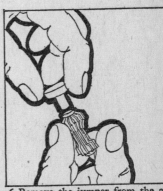

6 Remove the jumper from the anti-splash. If this is tight, lever it out carefully with a screwdriver.

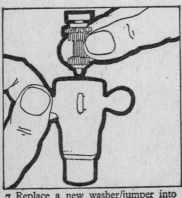

7 Replace a new washer/jumper into the anti-splash.

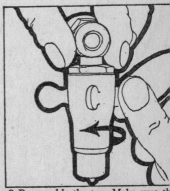

8 Reassemble the tap. Make sure that the anti-splash unit is correctly located. Screw nozzle back. Tighten gland nut.

a leaking gland nut

Water trickling from the top of the tap shield shows that the gland nut is loose, or that the packing needs renewing. For this repair you do not have to turn off the main stop valve and you will need an adjustable spanner, a screwdriver, an adjustable wrench, some petroleum jelly and adhesive tape.

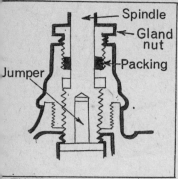

1 This shows a cross-section of a tap and the position of the gland nut packing.

2 If water seeps from around the top shield every time you turn on the tap, you must look to the gland nut or packing.

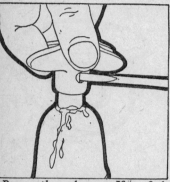

3 Remove the grub screw. If you find the capstan-type head stiff, tap it lightly upwards to remove verdigris and scale.

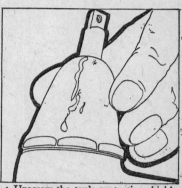

4 Unscrew the tap's protective shield. If tight, bind with adhesive tape and use an adjustable wrench, with care. Don't chip chrome.

5 Remove shield completely and the gland nut will be exposed.

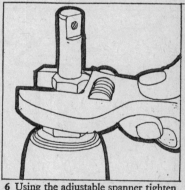

6 Using the adjustable spanner tighten the nut with a quarter turn. Temporarily replace capstan head and turn on water.

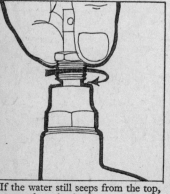

7 If the water still seeps from the top, remove the gland nut.

8 Dig out all loose packing. Rewind string well smeared with petroleum jelly round the spindle. Use screwdriver to press coil down evenly. Now re-assemble the tap.

replacing a cracked w.c. pan

W.C. pans are usually strongly built, but they do crack sometimes and need replacing. Here's how to take out your old pan and put in a new one.

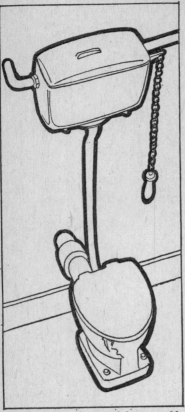

1 Cracks have developed in your old w.c. pan and it is time for a new one to be fitted.

2 If the cistern has its own stop tap turn it off. Otherwise turn off the mains' tap. Flush the cistern.

3 Remove the seat from the old pan. Try to pump the water in the pan dry. Tie some old rags to a stick for this job.

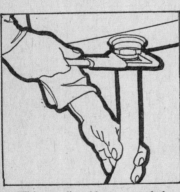

4 With an adjustable spanner slacken off the flush pipe nut under the cistern.

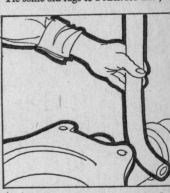

5 Put a sheet of polythene on the floor to save drips. Ease the flush pipe out of the rubber joining spigot on the pan.

6 Screws usually hold the pan to the floor. If difficult to remove, break the pan round them.

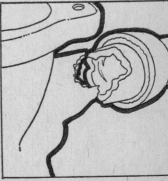

7 Break the outlet very carefully where it joins into the soil pipe. Great care should be taken here, whether dealing with 'P' or 'S' traps.

8 Stuff the soil pipe with old rags to prevent any debris going down the soil pipe and causing a blockage.

9 Chisel very carefully the remains of the pan spigot and jointing compound. Don't damage the soil pipe.

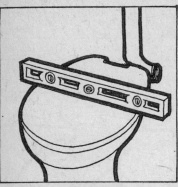

10 Remove rag plug from soil pipe and thoroughly dry the soil pipe socket. Try new pan into place—its spigot must be central in the socket of the soil pipe. Seat pan on bed of putty. Ensure it is level. Screw firmly to floor.

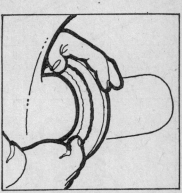

11 Joint the spigot to the soil pipe. Insert a hemp collar or gasket. Push this in until it meets the collar on the soil pipe. Pan spigot should also lightly touch this collar.

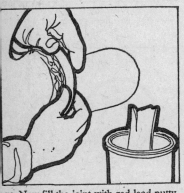

12 Now fill the joint with red lead putty or Plumber's Mate and trim to an angle. Leave to set for about eight hours.

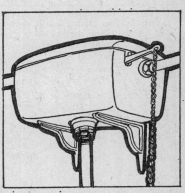

13 With adjustable spanner tighten back the flange nut connecting the flush pipe to the cistern.

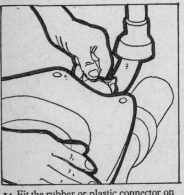

14 Fit the rubber or plastic connector on the flush pipe over the flushing horn of the pan. Wire it or use a waterproof sealing compound.

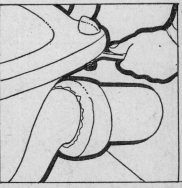

15 Fix on the seat taking care not to over-tighten the nuts. Flush the cistern several times and check all round joints for any leaks.

renewing a worn diaphragm

If you just get a trickle of water or none at all from your cistern, this faulty flushing is usually from an old type of cast iron bell-shaped syphon. But it can occur in a modern type of plastic syphon box. For the former a complete replacement may be necessary but for the modern type it may only be necessary to remove the diaphragm which has worn.

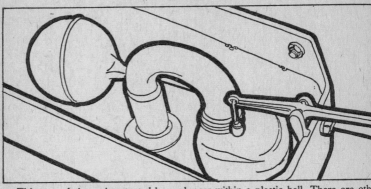

1 This type of cistern is actuated by a plunger within a plastic bell. There are other designs, but all work on the same principle.

2 Turn off the main water supply and flush the cistern until empty. OR you can tie up the ball valve after emptying.

3 Unscrew retaining nut from the flush pipe.

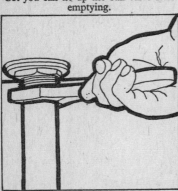

4 Unscrew the flange nut from under the cistern with an adjustable spanner.

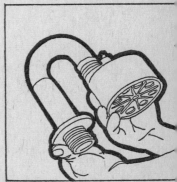

5 Remove handle and connecting rod from the syphon box. Take out the whole unit. Be sure to remove the retaining flush pipe washer.

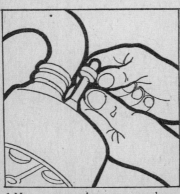

6 Now remove the spacer washers from the top of the plunger shaft.

7 Take out the plunger from the syphon bell chamber.

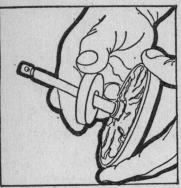

8 Remove the weight from the spindle of the plunger.

9 Remove worn diaphragm now revealed Clean the plunger well where hard water has formed salt deposits.

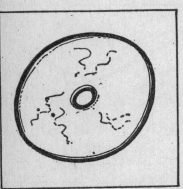

10 Buy an identical sized diaphragm from your local dealer.

11 Place the new diaphragm on the plunger.

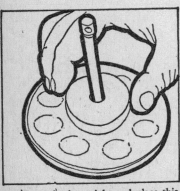

12 De-scale the weight and place this back into position.

13 Thoroughly clean the syphon box and replace the plunger.

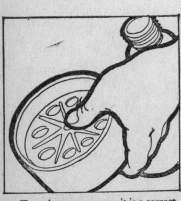

14 Test plunger to ensure it is a correct fit, neither undersize nor oversize.

15 Replace spacer washers. Reassemble back into the cistern. Join up the connecting rod and handle. Replace flange nut to flush pipe. Test cistern.

fitting a new gutter in plastic

Shown here are the various stages in replacing your old worn iron gutter with a plastic or PVC one. Plastic rain water pipes are easy to work with and are weather and rot proof.

1 Follow the makers' instruction leaflets for certain dimensions and adhesives and for general notes. Fix one gutter bracket at the down pipe end and the other bracket at the opposite end to the down pipe. Lay a string line between them to obtain the required slope.

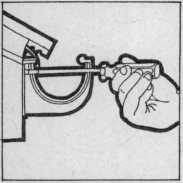

2 Secure the high point bracket as close as possible to the underside of the roofing felt and projecting tile.

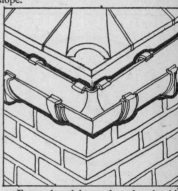

3 External and internal angles should have close supporting brackets on either side of the joints.

4 Fit close supporting brackets on either side of the gutter outlet.

5 This stop-end outlet must also be fitted with close supporting brackets.

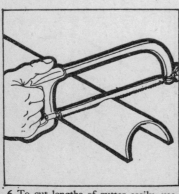

6 To cut lengths of gutter easily, use a fine tooth saw. Cut straight and square.

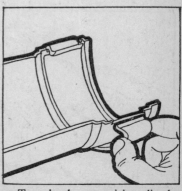

7 To make the gutter joint, clip the strap round the socket of a length of gutter into one of the notches.

8 In some gutter systems, the spigot needs a notch to mate with the socket. File this slot as shown to dimensions indicated by the manufacturers.

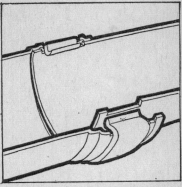

9 Turn the spigot end into the socket under the back edge of the strap so that the projection is between the notch.

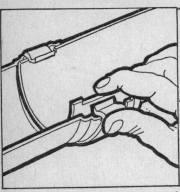

10 Ease front edge of spigot end down until it snaps under the strap, to compress gutter against the rubber seal and form a waterproof joint.

11 To fit the down pipe, fit the socket of the swan neck over the nozzle of the gutter outlet and the lower end into the socket of a rainwater pipe. Fasten pipe clip round the socket.

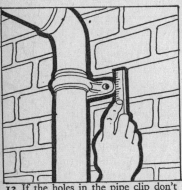

12 If the holes in the pipe clip don't line up with the mortar joint, measure the amount of spigot to be cut off in order to fix the pipe clip to the next mortar joint up.

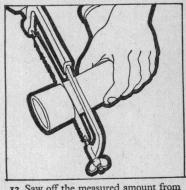

13 Saw off the measured amount from the swan neck spigot.

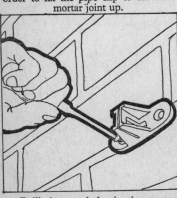

14 Drill the two holes in the mortar joint, plug and screw the back plate into position.

15 Replace swan neck and pipe, strap over socket and securely bolt up. New guttering is now complete.

fitting a plastic wastetrap

Plastic plumbing is so simple to use and is quick and easy to install. It is leak proof and does not corrode.

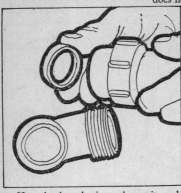

1 Here is the plastic outlet unit and neoprene ring giving a compression joint.

2 Apply some sealing compound to the underside of the waste flange.

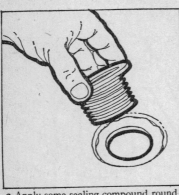

3 Apply some sealing compound round the sink hole and press the waste flange firmly in. Tightly screw up flange nut from below and allow to set.

4 Offer up the trap. Screw tightly to the flange screw projection, ensuring that the outlet lines up with the outside hole.

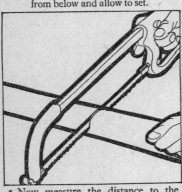

5 Now measure the distance to the outside hole from the U trap thread. Cut pipe to size.

6 Fit the neoprene sealing ring and loose nut, connect up to screwed thread of the U trap, screw up finger tight.

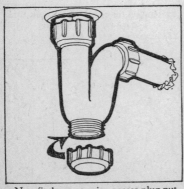

7 Now fit the waste pipe access plug nut into place.

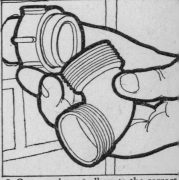

8 Connect the 90° elbow to the correct angle for the final pipe down to the drain. Make good round the hole on the wall with cement.

panelling in a bath

The appearance of a bath is greatly improved if it is panelled. You can clad the bath with a number of materials such as oil tempered hardboard or plastic coated boards, some with tile effects. The panels should be fastened with round headed screws and cupwashers for the easy removal of a panel to give access to the plumbing.

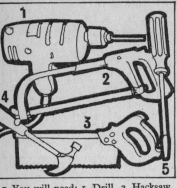

1 You will need: *1*. Drill. *2*. Hacksaw. *3*. Tenon saw. *4*. Hammer. *5*. Screwdriver.

2 Measure width and length of bath from each wall, also height from floor to under bath's rim. Allow measurements to take in pipes. Mark on wall and floor in pencil.

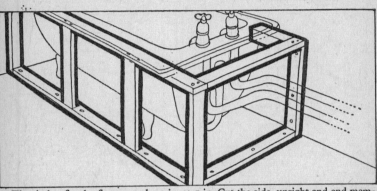

3 The timber for the frame can be 2 in. × 1 in. Cut the side, upright and end members. Nail or screw two uprights to each wall first. Nail or screw the bottom rails to the floor following the pencil marks, then the upper rails with uprights. Give the upper rail a tight fit under the rim of the bath. Screw all joints strongly.

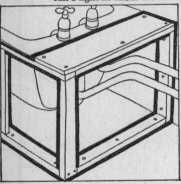

4 Now fit a top panel of plywood to nearly the height of the bath rim. Screw to side members. Make joint between bath and panel watertight with plastic sealing compound.

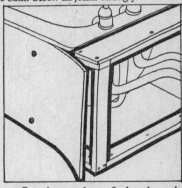

5 Cut the panels to fit length, end, and plywood top. Screw these to the vertical uprights with chrome round headed screws and cupwashers.

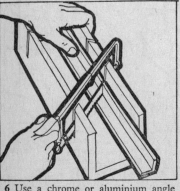

6 Use a chrome or aluminium angle strip to mask the joints of hardboard. Using a mitre board and hacksaw cut to the required height and width. Screw into position.

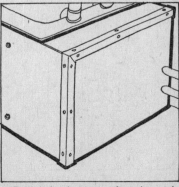

7 Drill holes in the angle strips and screw them to the hardboard and into the wood frame.

enamelling a bath

Painting a new bath needs a good deal of patience and care. Sometimes only a small part of a bath has flaked off, so the complete treatment would not be necessary.

WARNING: Make absolutely sure that the bath is free from dust and fluff before beginning painting.

1 You will need: *1*. Tin of bath enamel. *2*. Sponge. *3*. Wet and dry paper. *4*. 2 good soft brushes. *5*. White spirit. *6*. 2 small empty tins.

2 Remove the bath plug and chain to prevent them obstructing your painting. Sponge down bath with hot water and detergent.

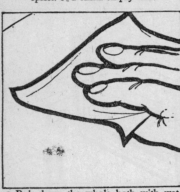

3 Rub down the whole bath with wet and dry dipped in clean water to get rid of scratches or chips. Rinse and allow to dry.

4 Tie empty tins to taps with string to catch drips which could ruin your work. Wipe all surfaces with white spirit and dry with cloth.

5 You must now prepare the paint. Stir the enamel thoroughly and adhere to the manufacturer's instructions.

6 Apply first coat of enamel evenly and lay off well, starting from the bottom of the bath.

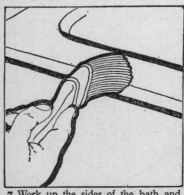

7 Work up the sides of the bath and finally the rim. Allow to dry for at least a day. Never lay off after the enamel begins to set otherwise patches will result.

8 Work the final coat quickly and evenly. Allow to dry for forty-eight hours. Then fill the bath with cold water and leave for another forty-eight hours to give the enamel good adhesion.

Miscellaneous Jobs

security in the home

Protecting your home and property is of the utmost importance to you and much can be done by the householder to prevent entry by the criminal. Fit good locks on doors and windows. This can easily be done at a small cost.

1 This Doormaster security chain will allow the door to be partially opened for checking callers.

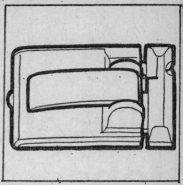

2 Ingersoll rim automatic deadlock which has a ten lever mechanism and is virtually unpickable.

3 Security bolt for wood doors or casement windows, stronger than surface bolts. Key is operated from inside only.

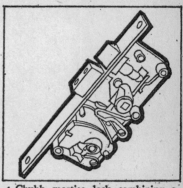

4 Chubb mortise lock combining a spring latch with a deadlock.

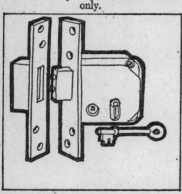

5 A Union five-lever mortise deadlock.

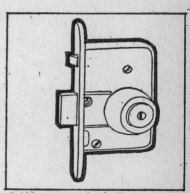

6 Abloy automatic deadlock mortise latch with single cylinder for solid doors and double for glass panelled doors.

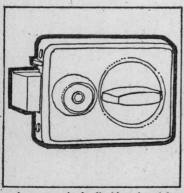

7 An automatic deadlocking rim night latch suitable for glass-panelled doors.

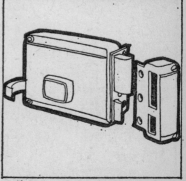

8 A Yale cylinder rim lock having a night latch combined with a deadlock used for solid or glass-panelled front doors.

9 A safety device, key operated which can be bolted easily to the handle of a metal casement window.

10 This device fits to the side rail of the top sash window and is key operated. (Sash-lok).

11 A key operated device with a threaded stay-pin for wooden casement windows, to prevent the stay being lifted off its pin. (Stay-lok).

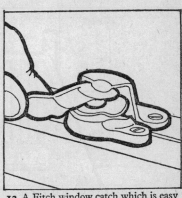

12 A Fitch window catch which is easy to fit and cannot be opened from the outside with a knife, etc.

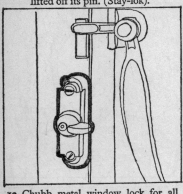

13 Chubb metal window lock for all metal casement windows. Fitted to the fixed frame of the window and key operated.

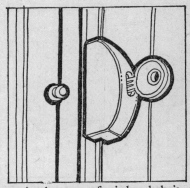

14 Another type of window lock is fitted with self-tapping screws for metal windows. Key operated.

15 This key operated window lock is for wooden windows or fanlights pivoted and top hung.

16 For sliding sash windows. Plate is fitted flush to top frame to secure window; chain fitted to surrounding frame of window. Allows ventilation while locked.

safety in the home

It is the duty of the householder to make sure that certain points are observed with regard to the risk of accidents. Below we show some of the things to be avoided.

1 Oil heaters should be fixed in some way to a wall or to the floor.

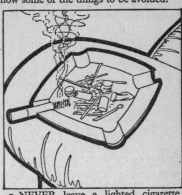

2 NEVER leave a lighted cigarette on an ashtray where it can fall out and cause a fire.

3 Try to position a light on the landing. Lack of light in this dark area can cause falls.

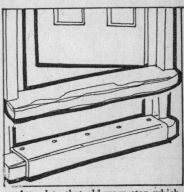

4 Attend to that old worn step which can cause someone to fall. Put a metal tread over the old step.

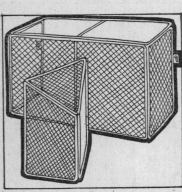

5 Guard all open fires. Use a fixed fire guard which conforms to British Standard regulations.

6 Avoid placing mirrors or pictures over a fireplace. Someone may get too close to take a look.

7 Avoid using long flexes. Better to have a point installed nearer the appliance. If you must extend a flex, use a proper connector.

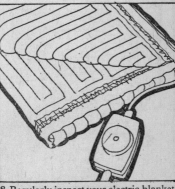

8 Regularly inspect your electric blanket for fraying of the cord. Have it serviced at least every other year, and store flat or rolled.

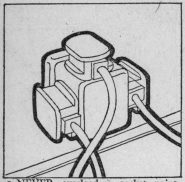

9 NEVER overload a socket point with too many appliances. This could easily result in a fire.

10 Handles of saucepans on the cooker should always be turned inwards, otherwise they could be pulled over and cause severe scalding.

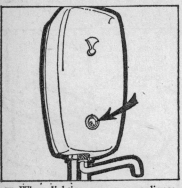

11 When lighting any gas appliance, ALWAYS have a light ready before turning on the gas.

12 NEVER drape the flex of an electrical appliance over a cooker. And never rest an electric kettle on the top of a gas cooker. You could absentmindedly light the gas beneath it.

13 Never have an electric fire or any other sort of portable equipment in the bathroom. This could be fatal.

14 Never leave flexes under a carpet. They can easily be kicked and the plug pulled out of the socket. Or worse, treading on the flex may damage it and a fire could result.

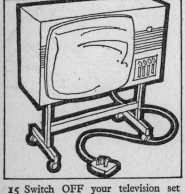

15 Switch OFF your television set when not in use and remove the plug from the mains socket.

16 DO NOT position an electric fire or any other portable fire near curtains, bedding, or furniture. Keep furniture a sensible distance from any heat source. ALWAYS unplug electric fires when not in use.

17 ALWAYS fill an oil stove out of doors and be careful not to overfill.

18 ON NO ACCOUNT move a lighted paraffin stove. This is HIGHLY DANGEROUS.

19 If a gas tap handle is detachable, remove it when not in use. Fold down hinged gas taps, so as to avoid kicking on the gas accidently.

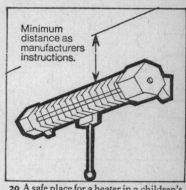

20 A safe place for a heater in a children's room or workshop is often the wall. But be careful to place it away from high furniture and inflammable materials.

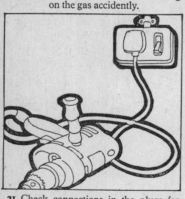

21 Check connections in the plugs for your power tools regularly. Use a fused plug and/or socket.

22 ALWAYS keep inflammable or poisonous materials and household chemicals in their original containers and well out of the reach of children. Lower cupboards containing harmful materials should be fitted with locks.

23 DO NOT leave wood shavings on the garage or workshop floor.

24 DON'T use a naked light in your garage, but use a protected hand-lamp, connected in accordance with the manufacturer's instructions.

sharpening jobs around the house

Constant use tends to blunt domestic cutting appliances and to restrict their usefulness. You can sharpen them quite easily. But remember, ALWAYS KEEP YOUR HANDS AWAY FROM THE EDGE YOU ARE SHARPENING.

WARNING: Always wear protective goggles when using a grindstone.

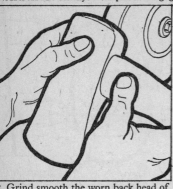

1 Grind smooth the worn back head of your axe and round it slightly to prevent a thick build up.

2 Lay the axe overhanging on a bench top. Work the oilstone across the blade inclined towards the edge until sharp. Repeat for other side.

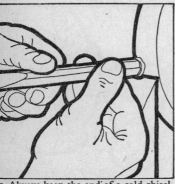

3 Always keep the end of a cold chisel free of burrs to prevent bits from flying off when hammering. Twist end of chisel against grindstone to remove them.

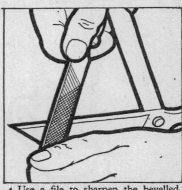

4 Use a file to sharpen the bevelled edges of your shears. Hold them in a vice and stroke away from you diagonally across edge.

5 To sharpen scissors, use an oilstone. Push the bevel of the blade forward with diagonal strokes.

6 To sharpen a penknife push one way at a shallow angle on the oilstone then rotate knife edge the other way.

7 Use a slipstone to sharpen lino cutting knives. Have the edge on the curve of the stone and stroke away from you.

8 A patent sharpener for kitchen and wavy edge knives. Draw the knife through the two hardened wheels towards you a number of times.

removing stains from fabrics

Stains must be dealt with promptly before they dry and set on fabrics. If you have the proper chemicals to hand you can get rid of certain stains. But of course some stains will need professional attention.

WARNING: Certain spirits and solvents are HIGHLY INFLAMMABLE and some give off poisonous fumes. Use cleaning spirits only in well ventilated rooms.

1 TEA: Soak in a hot solution of $\frac{1}{2}$ oz. borax to $\frac{1}{2}$ pt. of water then rinse in warm water.

2 COFFEE: Wash the article in 1 part household ammonia to 4 parts warm water then rinse in hot water.

3 BEER: Clean with a solution of one part sal ammoniac, one part 'meths' and four parts warm water.

4 WINE: Sponge or soak in acetic acid.

5 MILK: Soak the material in hot water containing biological washing powder.

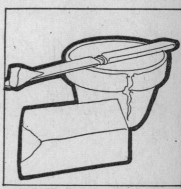

6 GREASE: Place a piece of blotting paper either side of the material. Press with a hot iron. Remove any traces with a proprietary grease solvent.

7 EGG: Dab spot with glycerine and leave. Mix a small amount of soft soap and 'meths'. Rub over spot. Rinse in warm water.

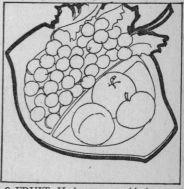

8 FRUIT: Hydrogen peroxide is usually effective, but may cause the material to bleach.

9 OIL: Place blotting paper under material and dab with a proprietary grease solvent.

10 TOBACCO: Rub a solution of 25 gm. sodium sulphite and 100 cc. of water on stained fingers. Wash off with soap and water.

11 NAIL VARNISH: Apply acetone to the spot. Remove any traces of colour left with 'meths'.

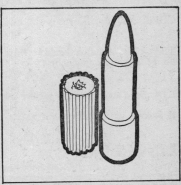

12 LIPSTICK: Rub with a proprietary grease solvent and finally hydrogen peroxide.

13 ICE CREAM: Sponge with warm soapy water. Rinse and dry.

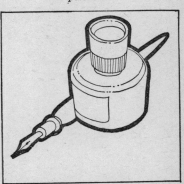

14 INK: Wet with solution of hydrogen peroxide and hold in steam until faded. Remove faded stain with solution of oxalic acid dissolved in water.

15 PAINT: Rub with benzene and 'meths'. If paint remains hard it is probably cellulose. Use acetone to remove it.

16 SHOE POLISH: Swab with a proprietary grease solvent and afterwards use methylated spirits.

removing stains from surfaces

BRICKWORK

For discolouration wash with soda soap. If the discolouration is smoky use a soap solution mixed with household ammonia. Clean off white encrustation with a wire brush and paint any remainder with spirits or salt. Leave to dry and wipe with clean water. If there is persistent discolouration it would be best to paint over with a brick coloured paint.

CONCRETE

For rust use a strong solution of oxalic acid painted on with a stiff brush. Wipe with clean water. If your concrete is a dirty colour, wash with soap and water. If the concrete doesn't come up clean, paint with cement paint.

WOOD

OIL: For oil stains use a talc paste or whiting and trisodium phosphate mixed with a little water. Leave on for as long as necessary.

PAINT: For paint stains scrape off all you can and use trisodium phosphate or a paint stripper. Scrape clean, then wash with water.

TAR: Try lifting tar stains with petrol or paraffin. Scrape off as much tar as you can then use a rag soaked in the spirit.

SCUFFS: Use a fine steel wool to take off scuff marks.

COFFEE: Wash coffee stains with soap and water. Carbon tetrachloride should remove stains left over.

TEA: A borax solution should get rid of tea stains. Leave this on and wipe off.
For general discolouration use strong oxalic acid solution and leave. This bleaches the wood. Wash well with water.

INK: Soap and water can remove ink stains. If not, try citric acid and leave for a quarter of an hour. Wash off with water.
If Stain is unidentifiable, scrub with fine steel wool. Seal exposed wood to match surrounds.

LINOLEUM

Scrape off stains carefully without causing any damage to the lino. Paint persistent stains with glycerine and leave for a quarter of an hour. If still persistent try 1 part ammonia to 2 parts carbon tetrachloride or 3 parts acetone but NEVER use strong alkaline cleaners or paint strippers on lino.